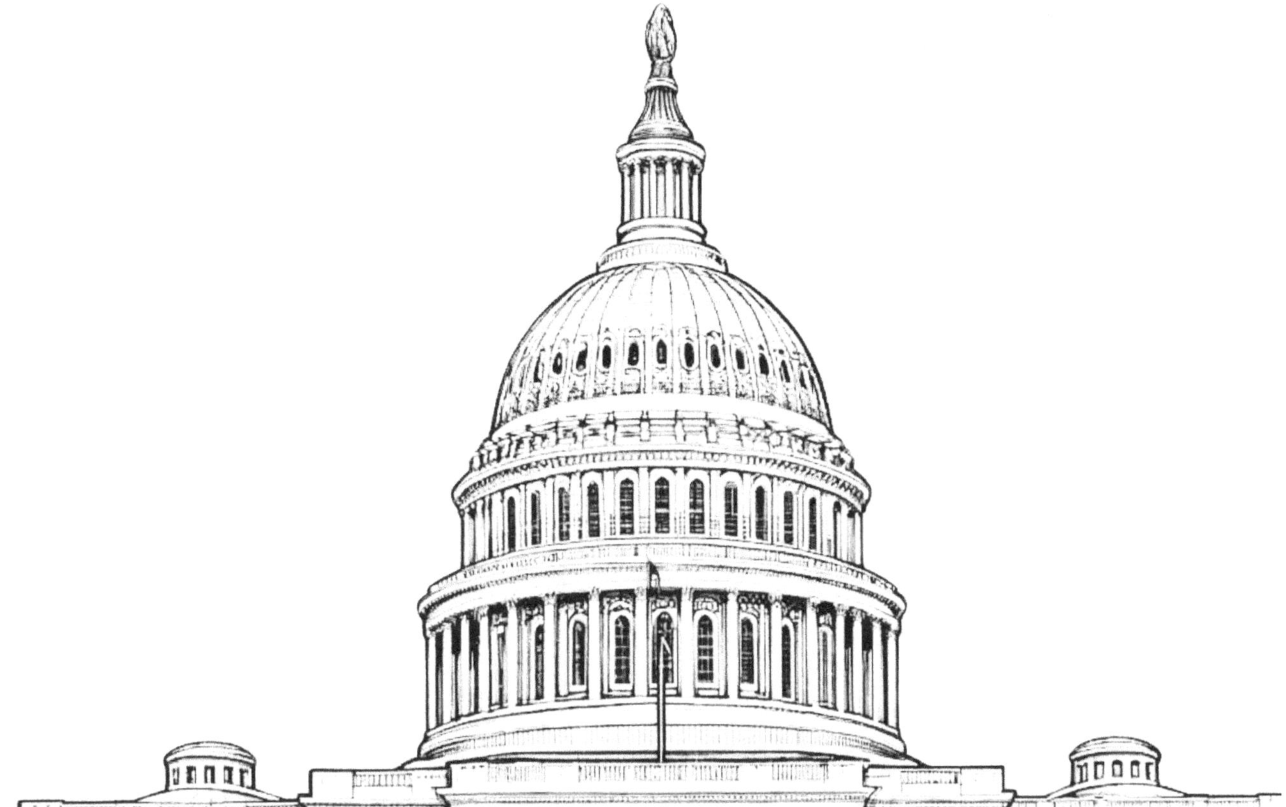

UNITED STATES CAPITOL, WASHINGTON

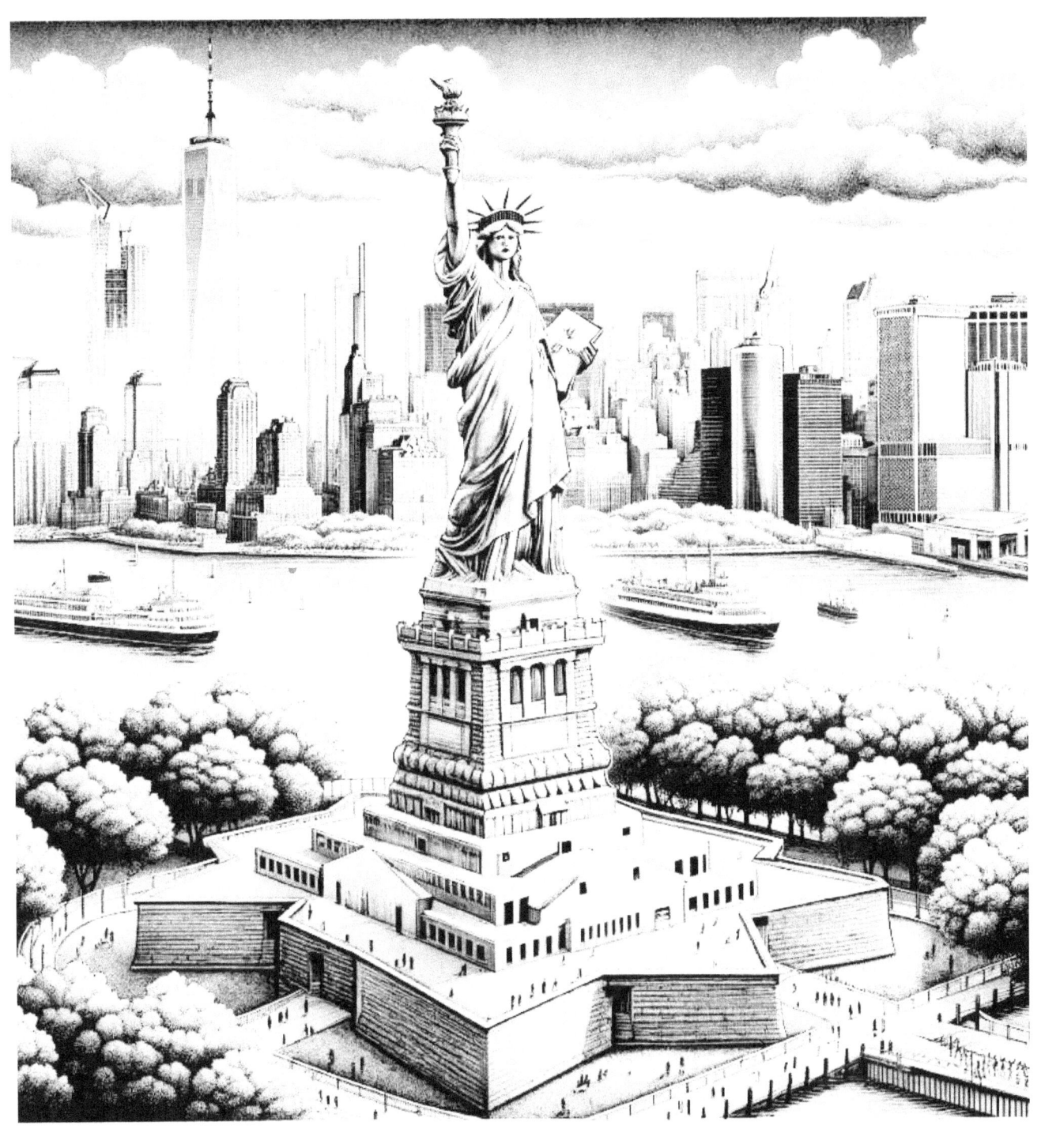

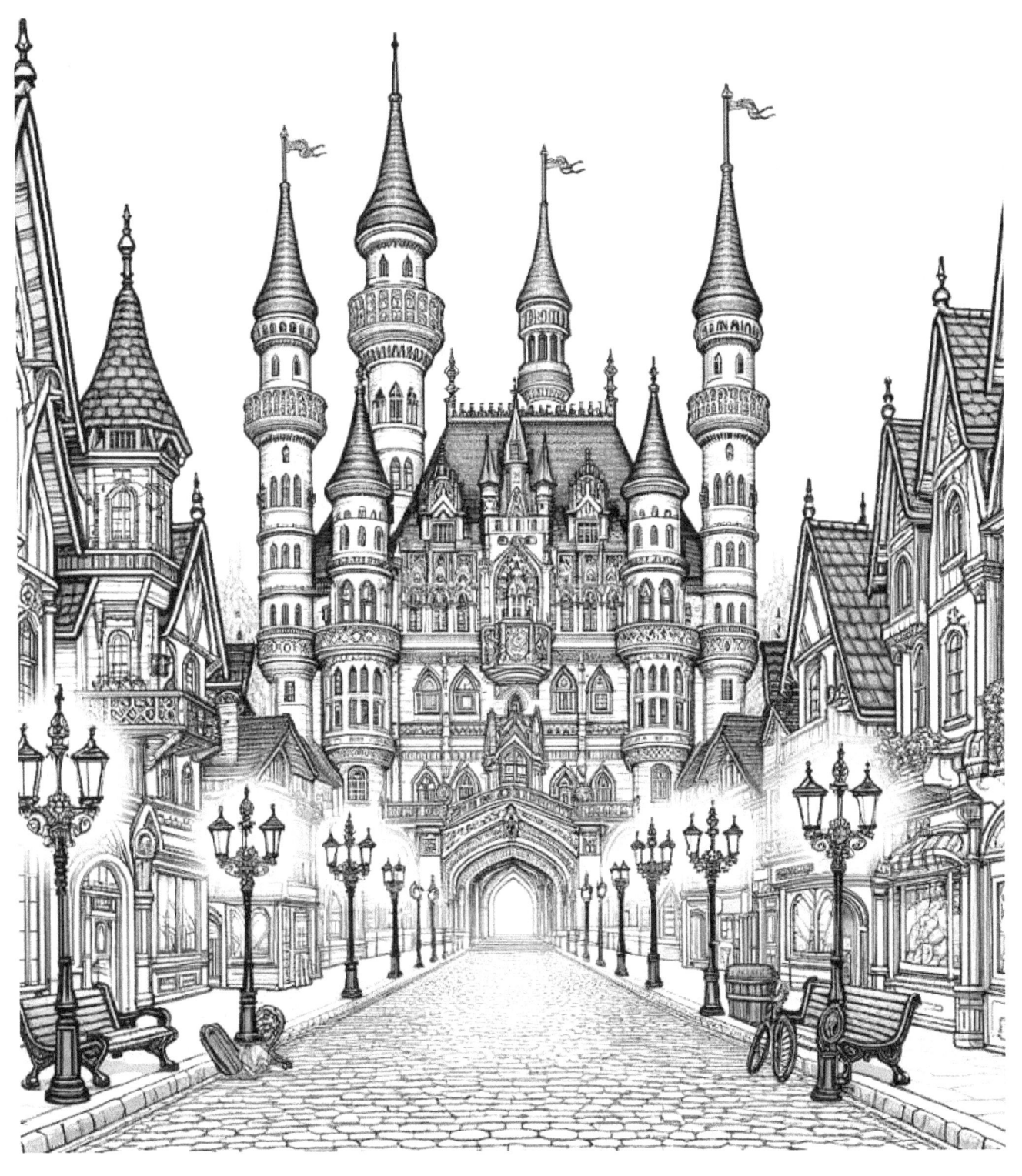

DISNEY WORLD, FLORIDA

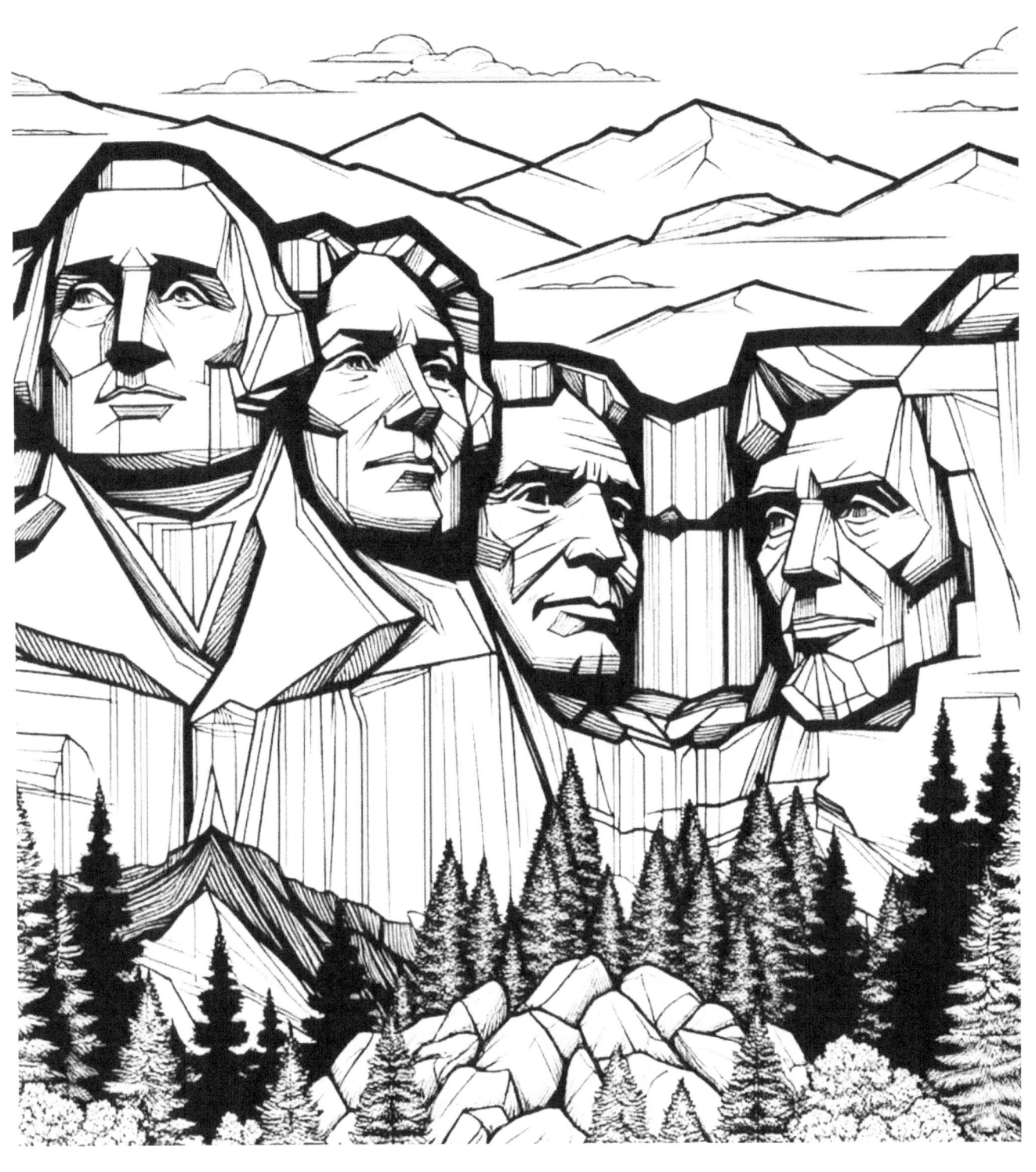

MOUNT RUSHMORE, SOUTH DAKOTA

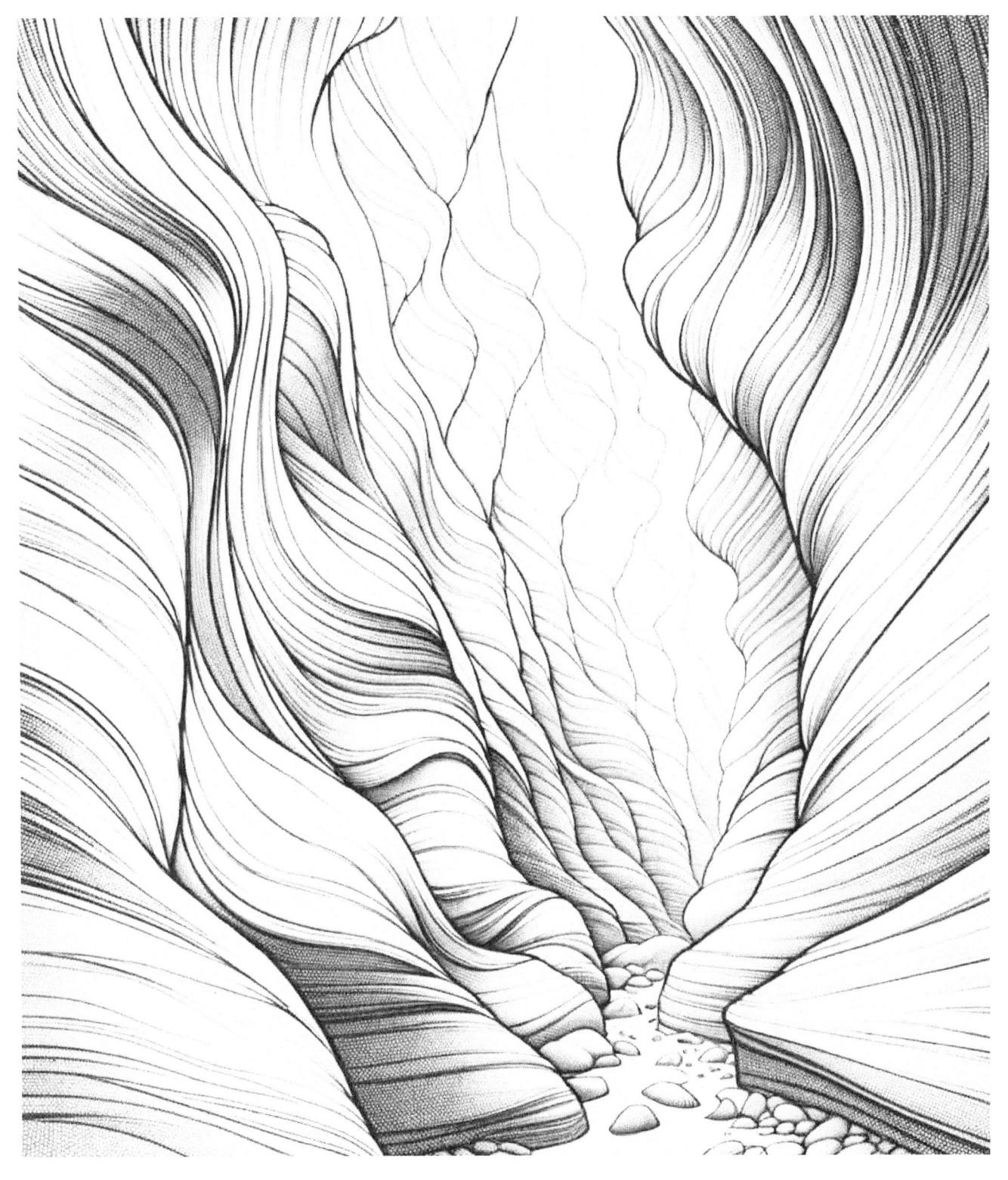

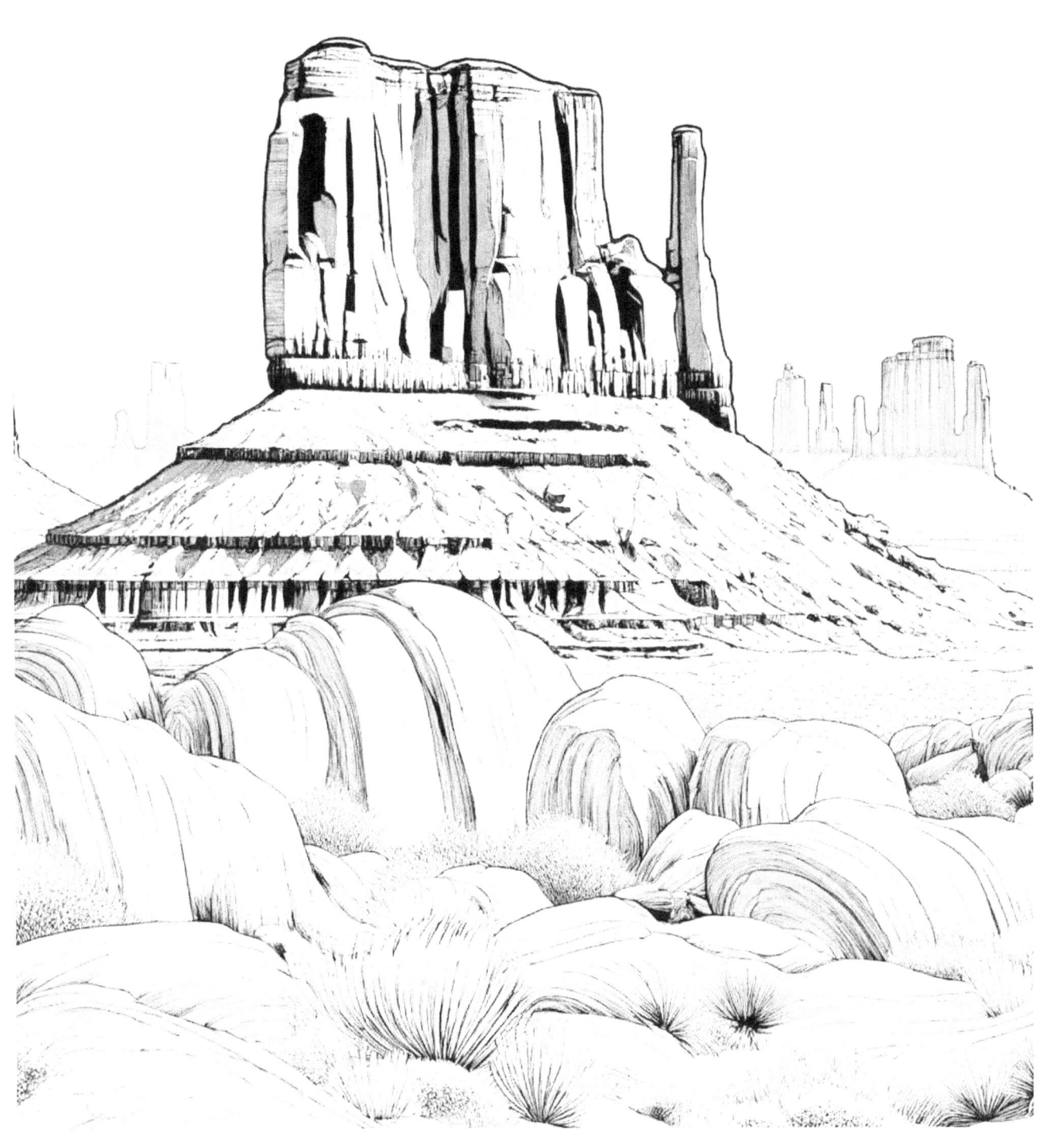

MONUMENT VALLEY, ARIZONA/

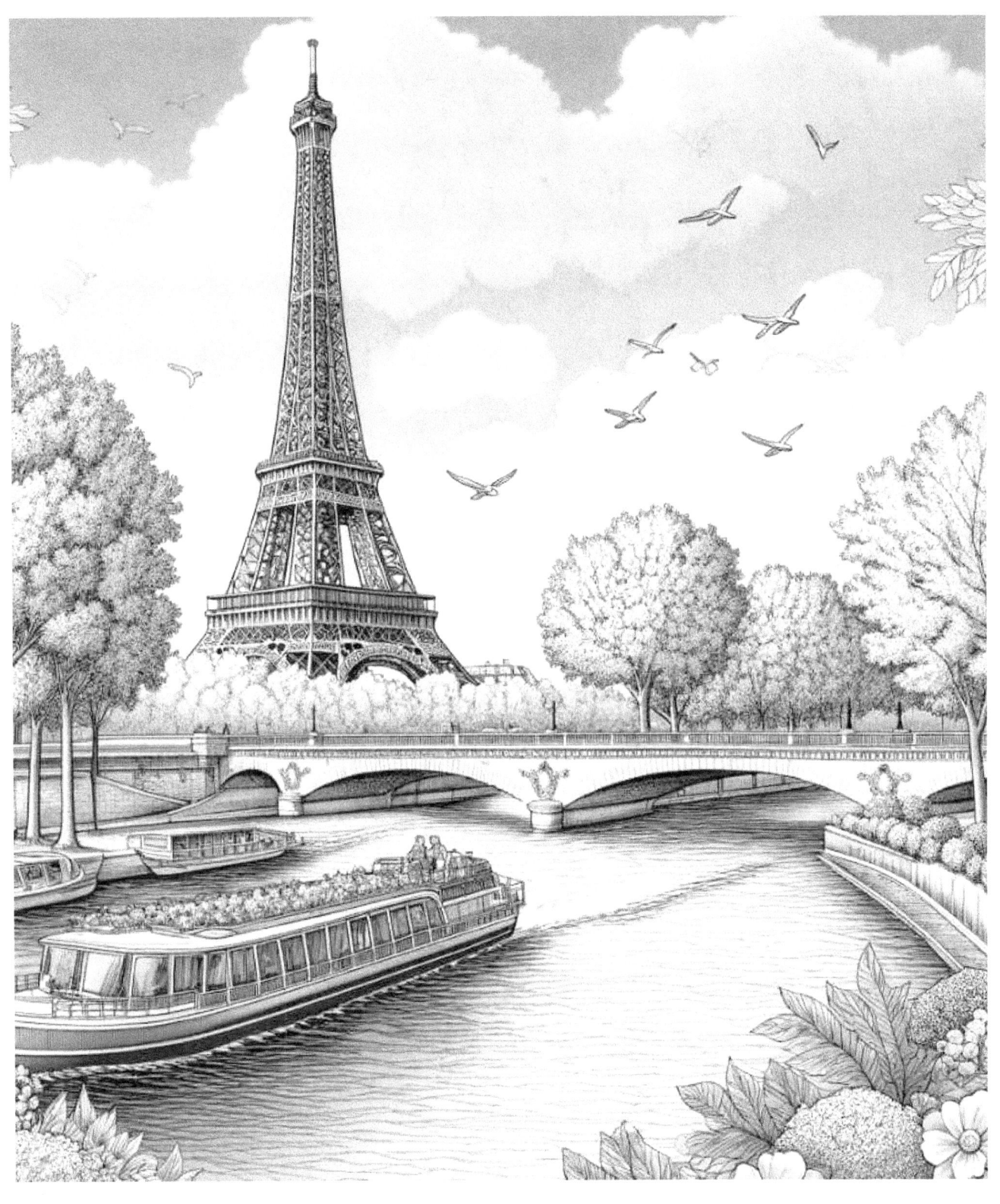

EIFFEL TOWER.PARIS

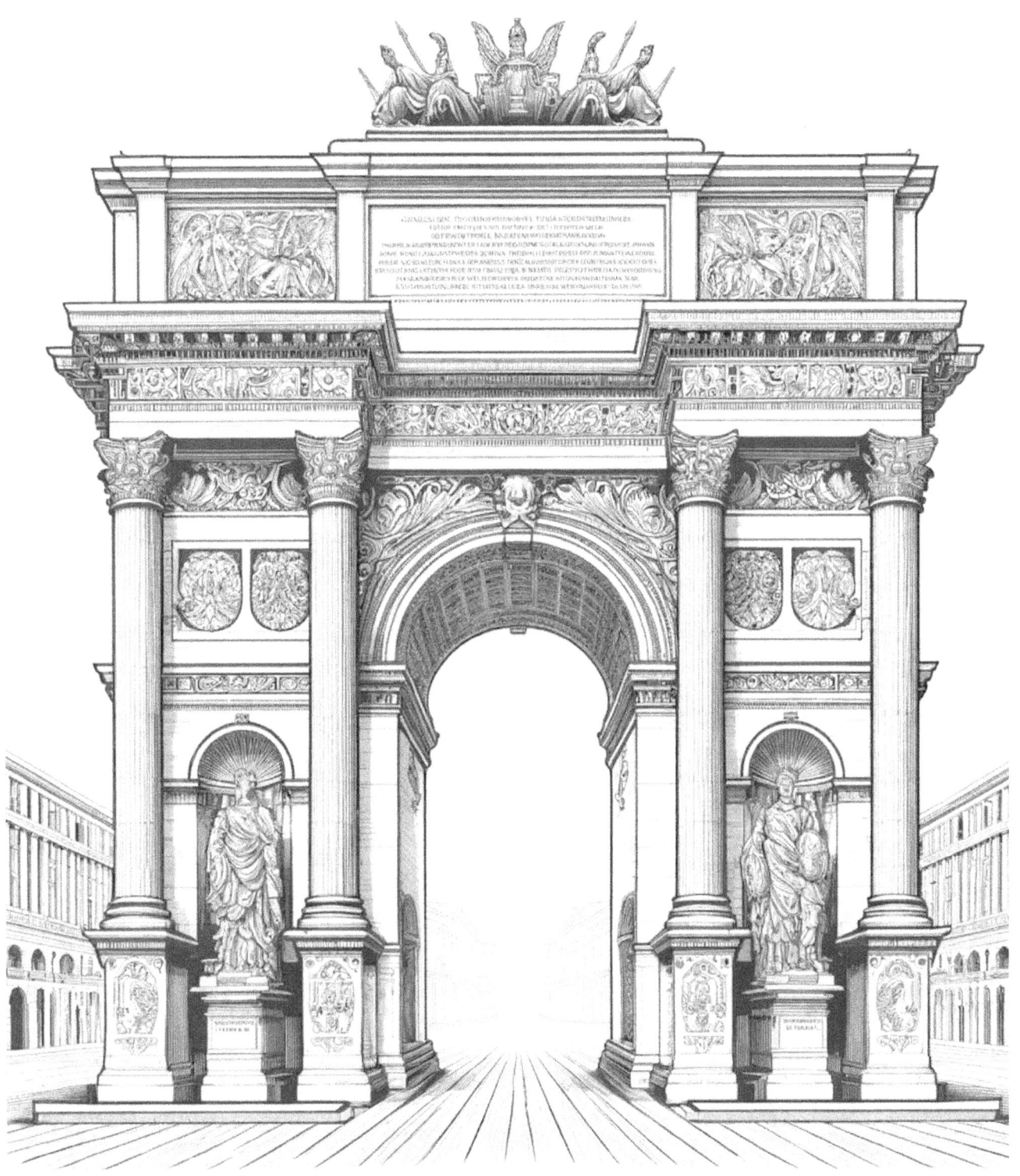

THE ARC DE TRIOMPHE.PARIS

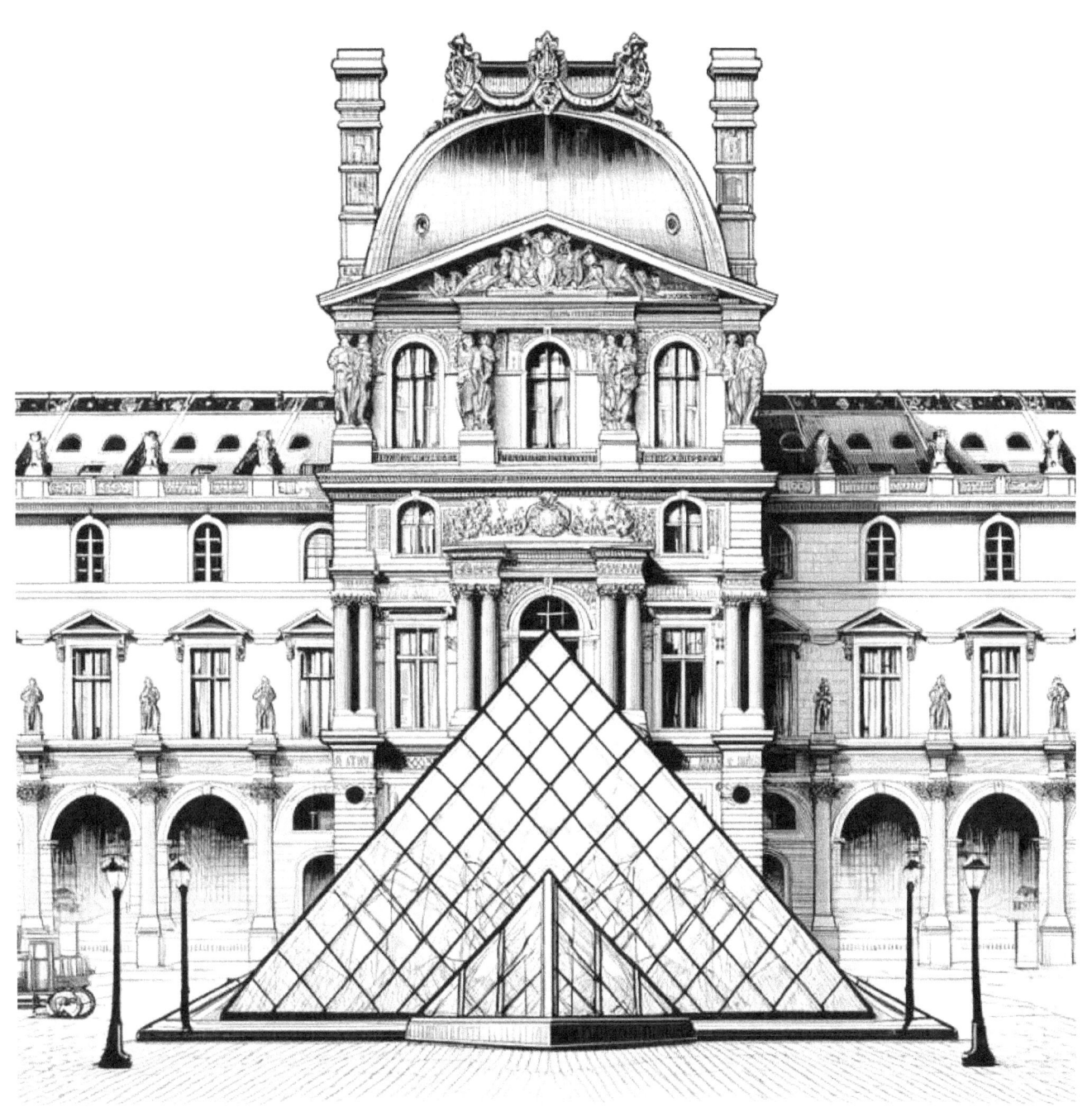

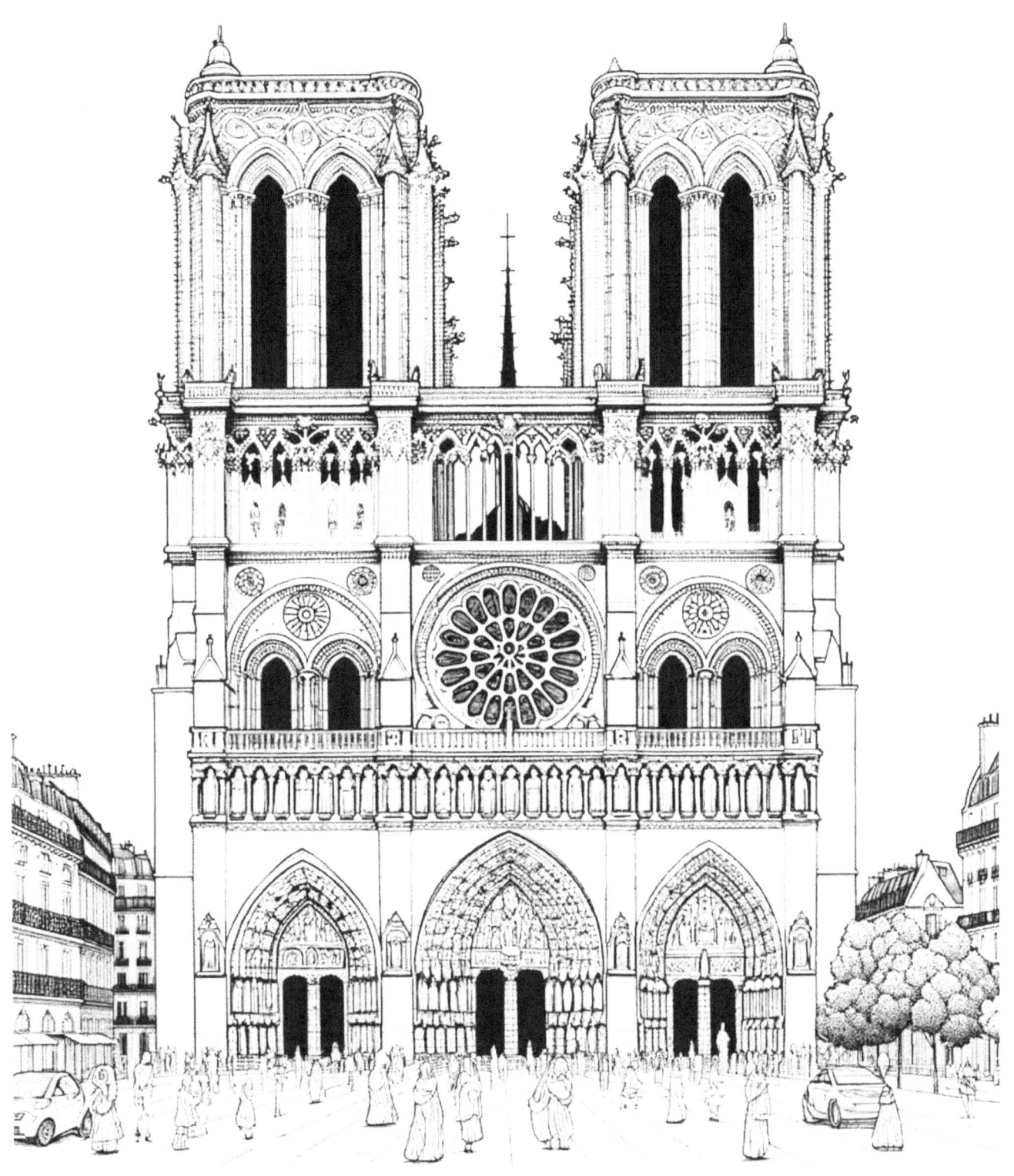

NOTRE DAME CATHEDRAL.PARIS

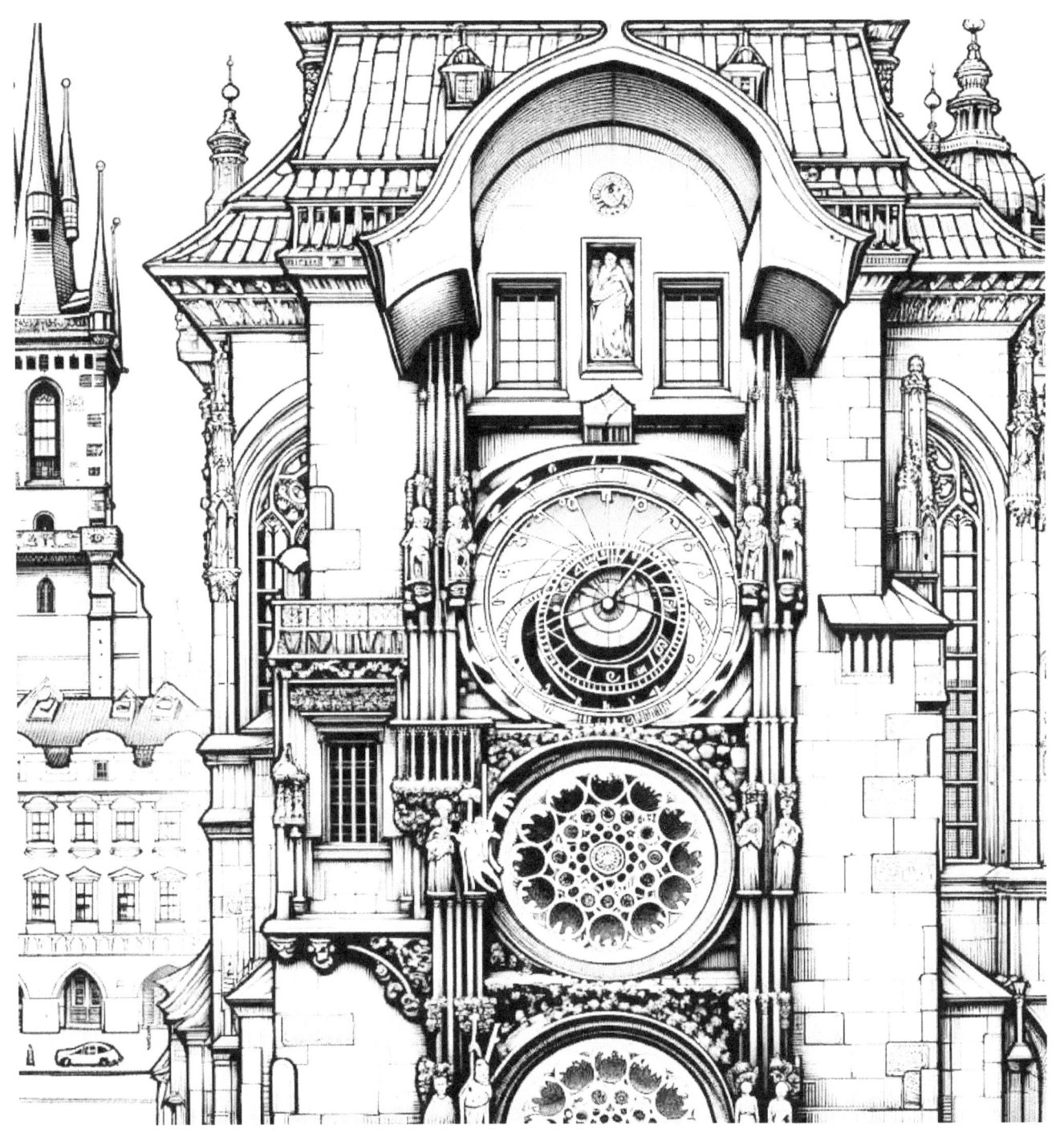

ASTRONOMICAL CLOCK.
PRAGUE

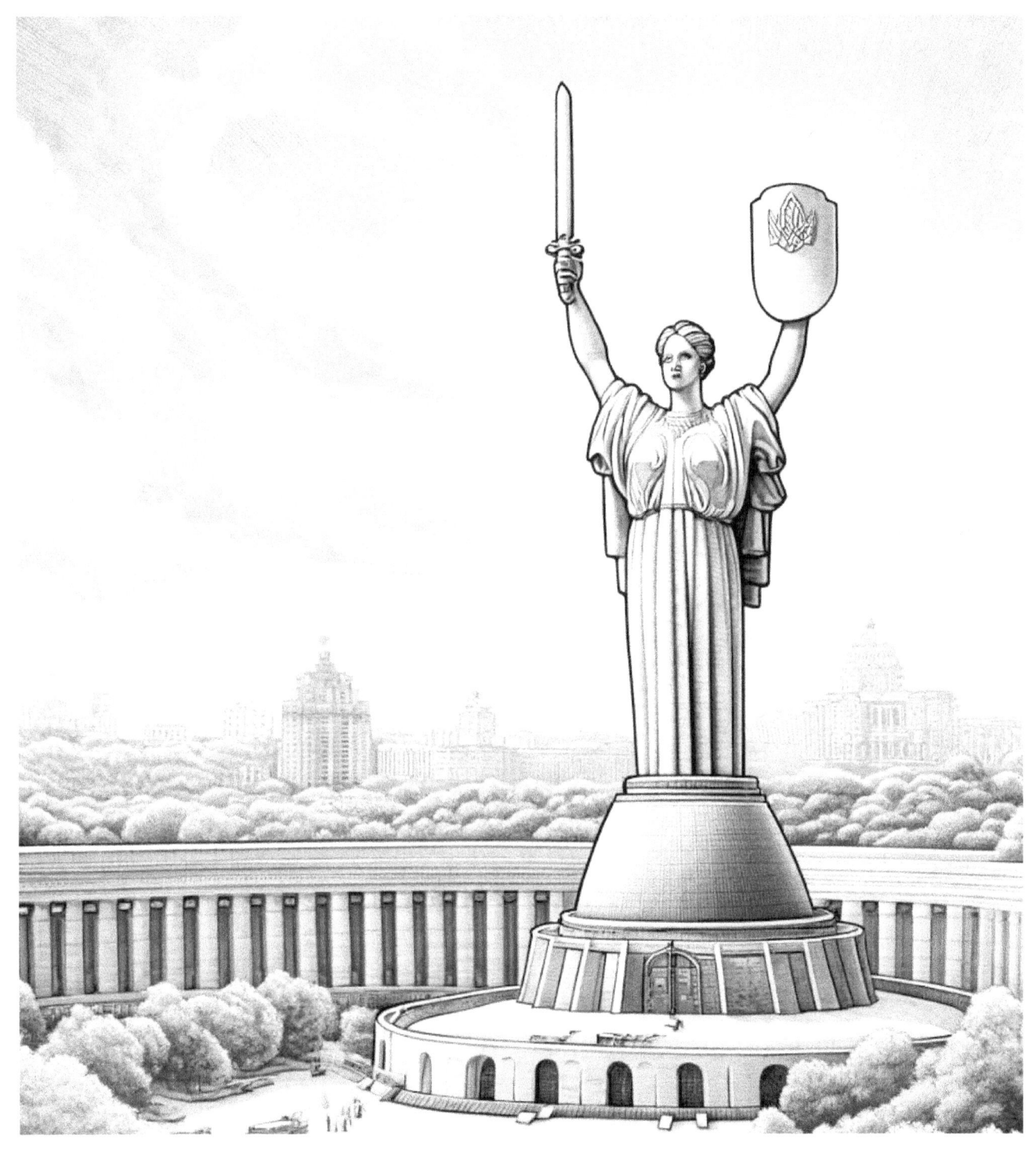

MOTHERLAND STATUE MONUMENT.KIEV

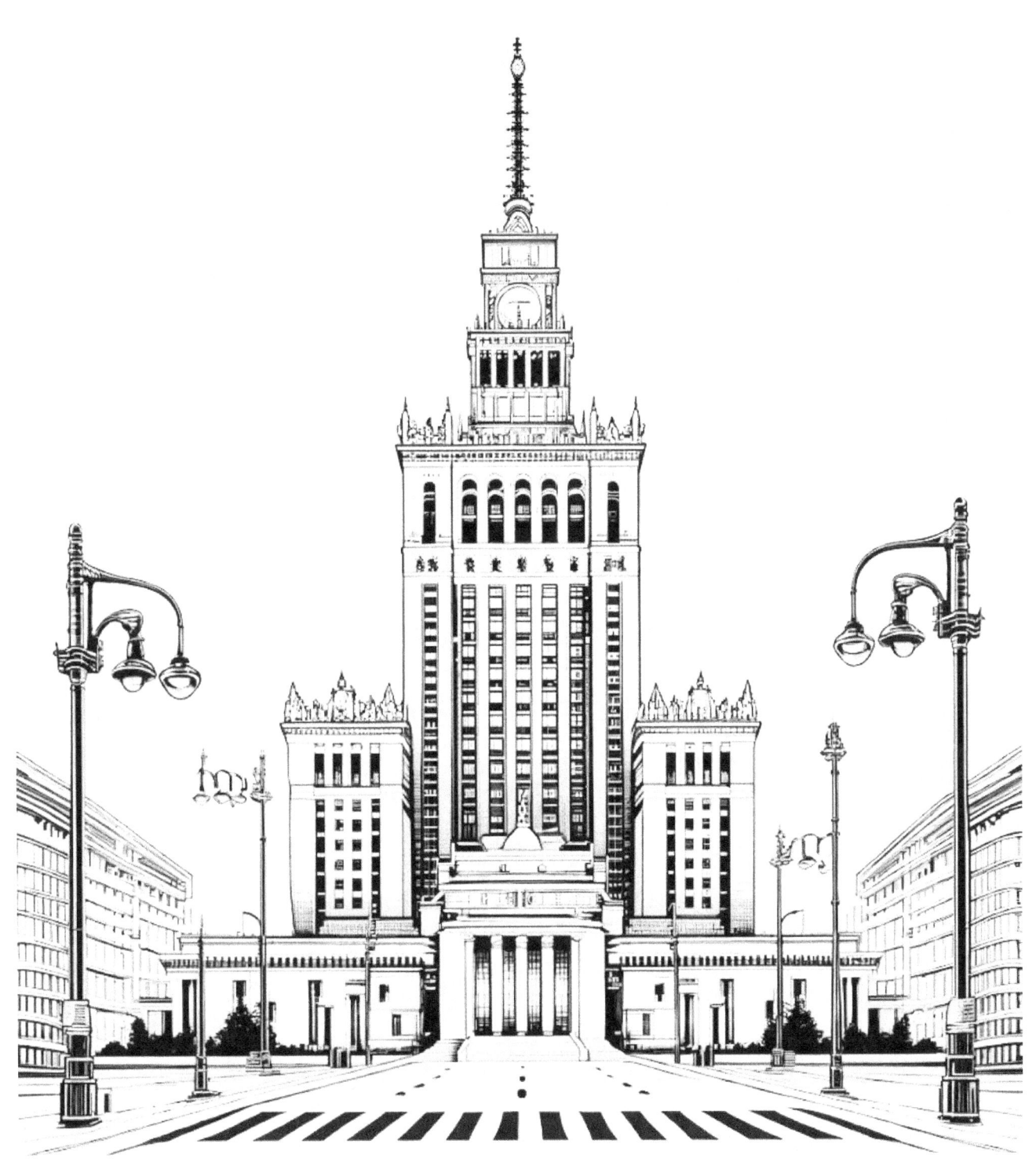

PALACE OF CULTURE
AND SCIENCE.WARSAW

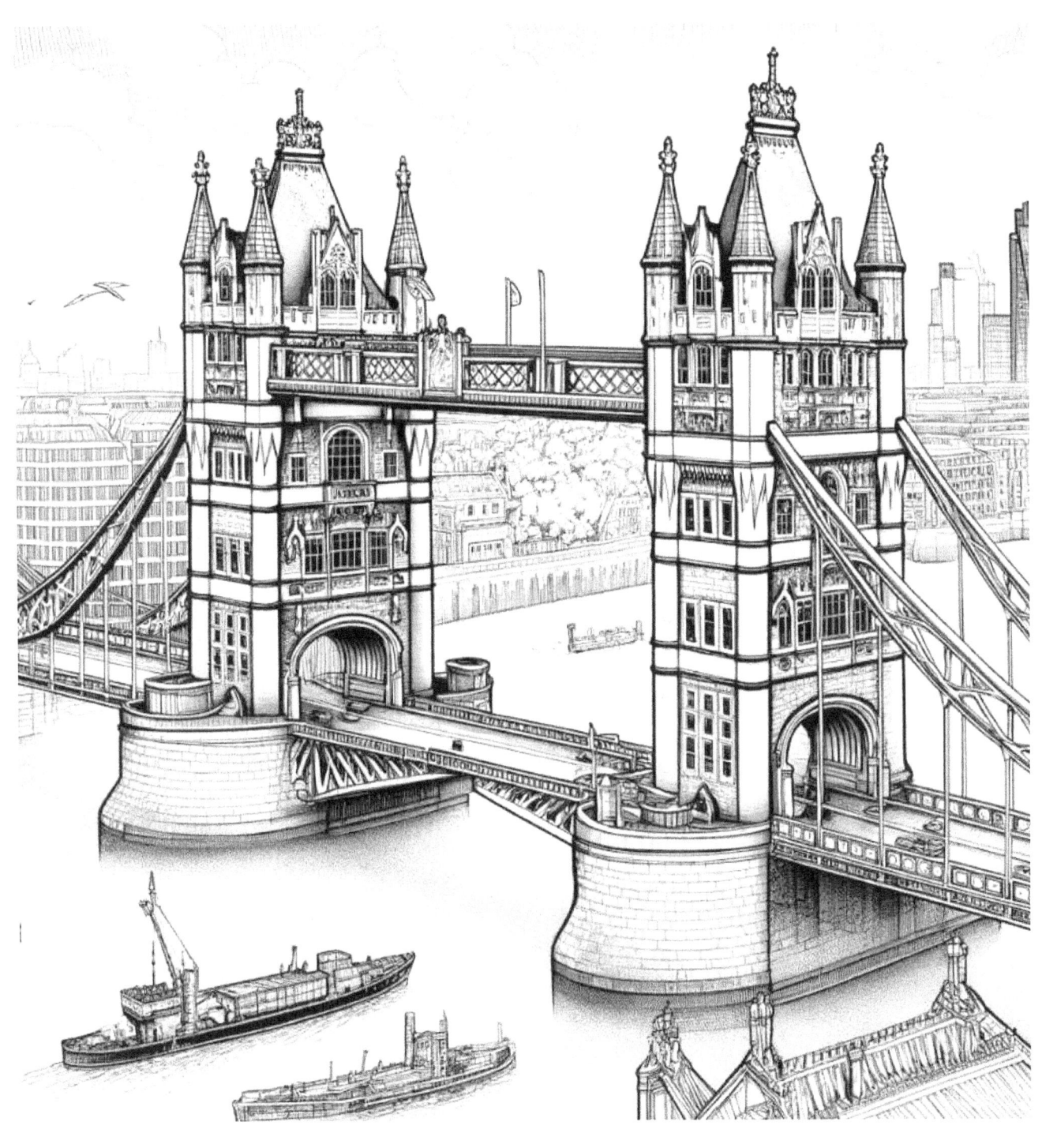

TOWER BRIDGE.LONDON

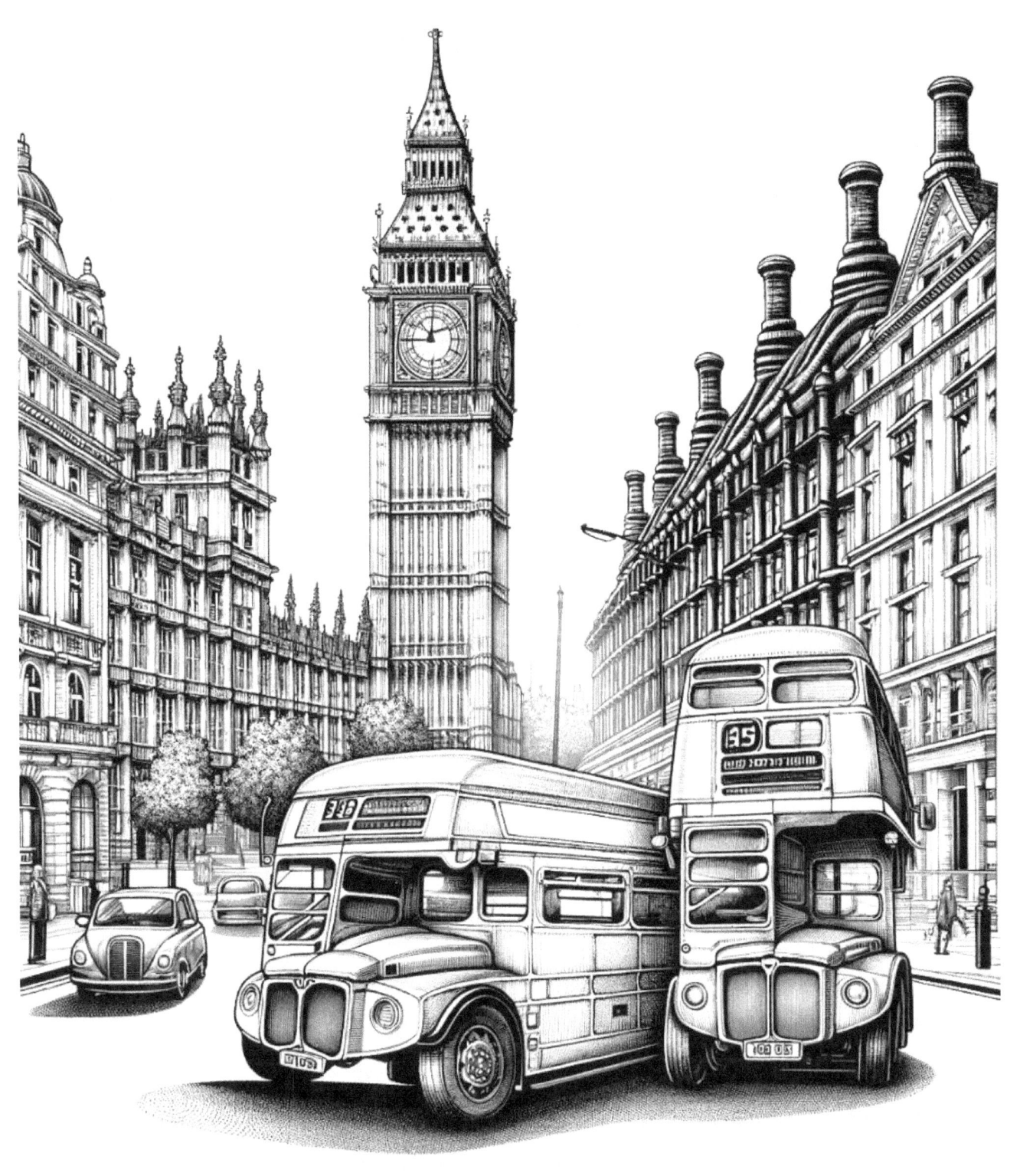

BIG BEN.LONDON

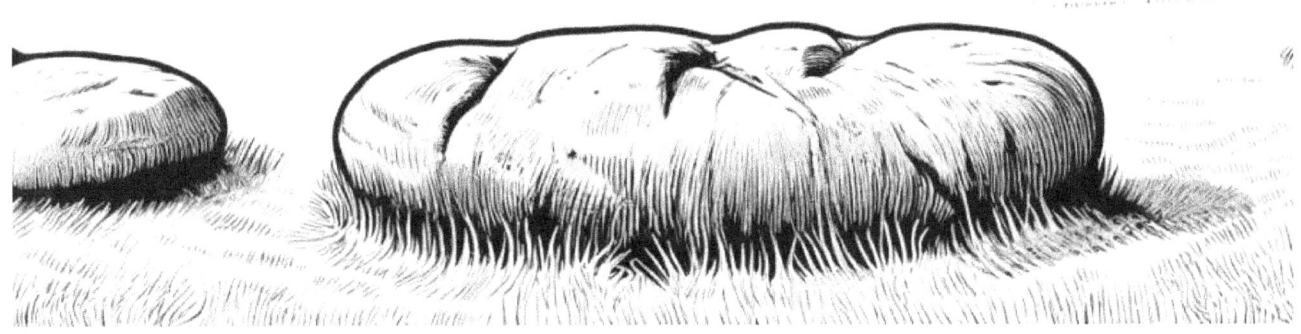

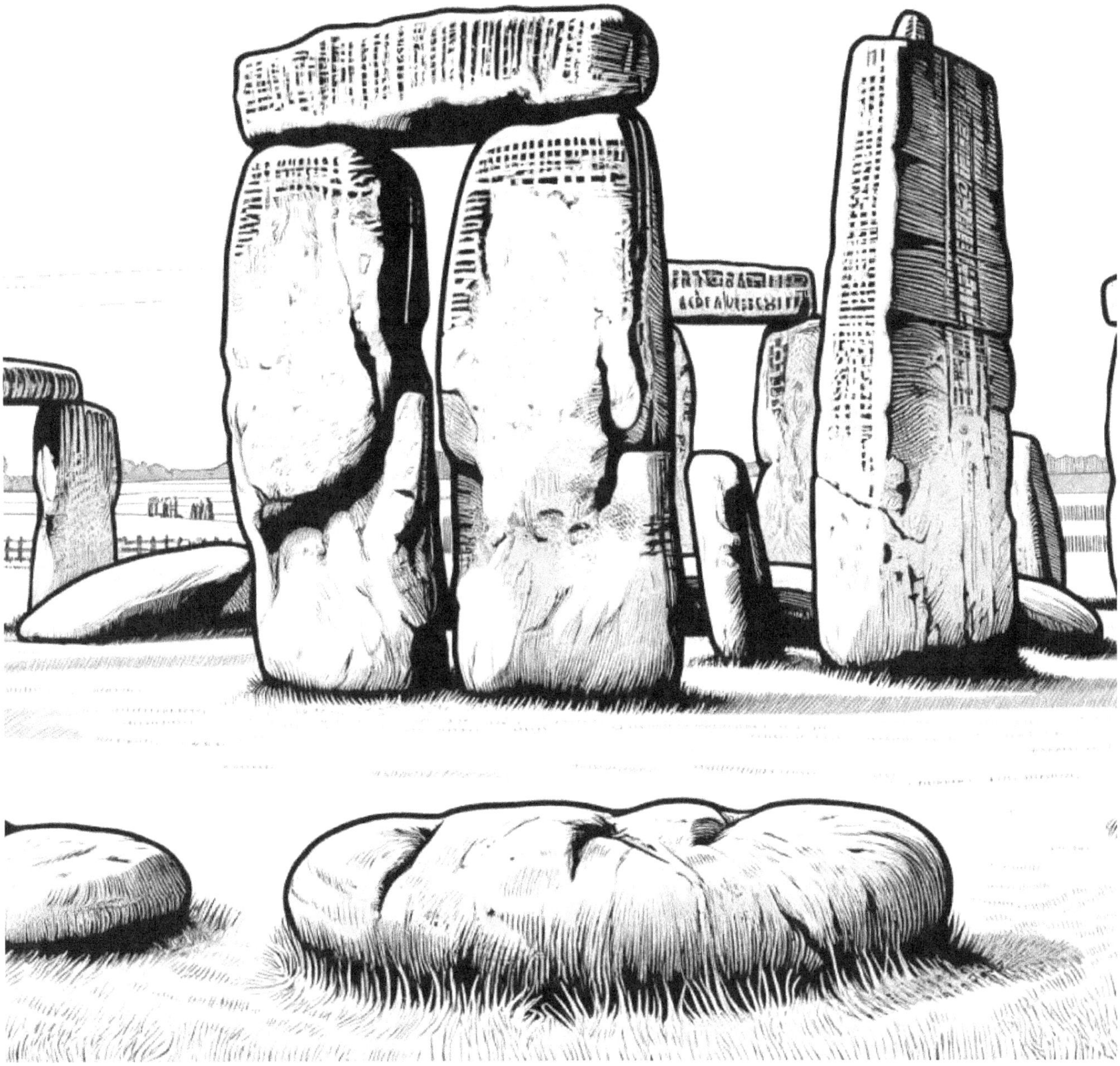

STONEHENGE.LONDON

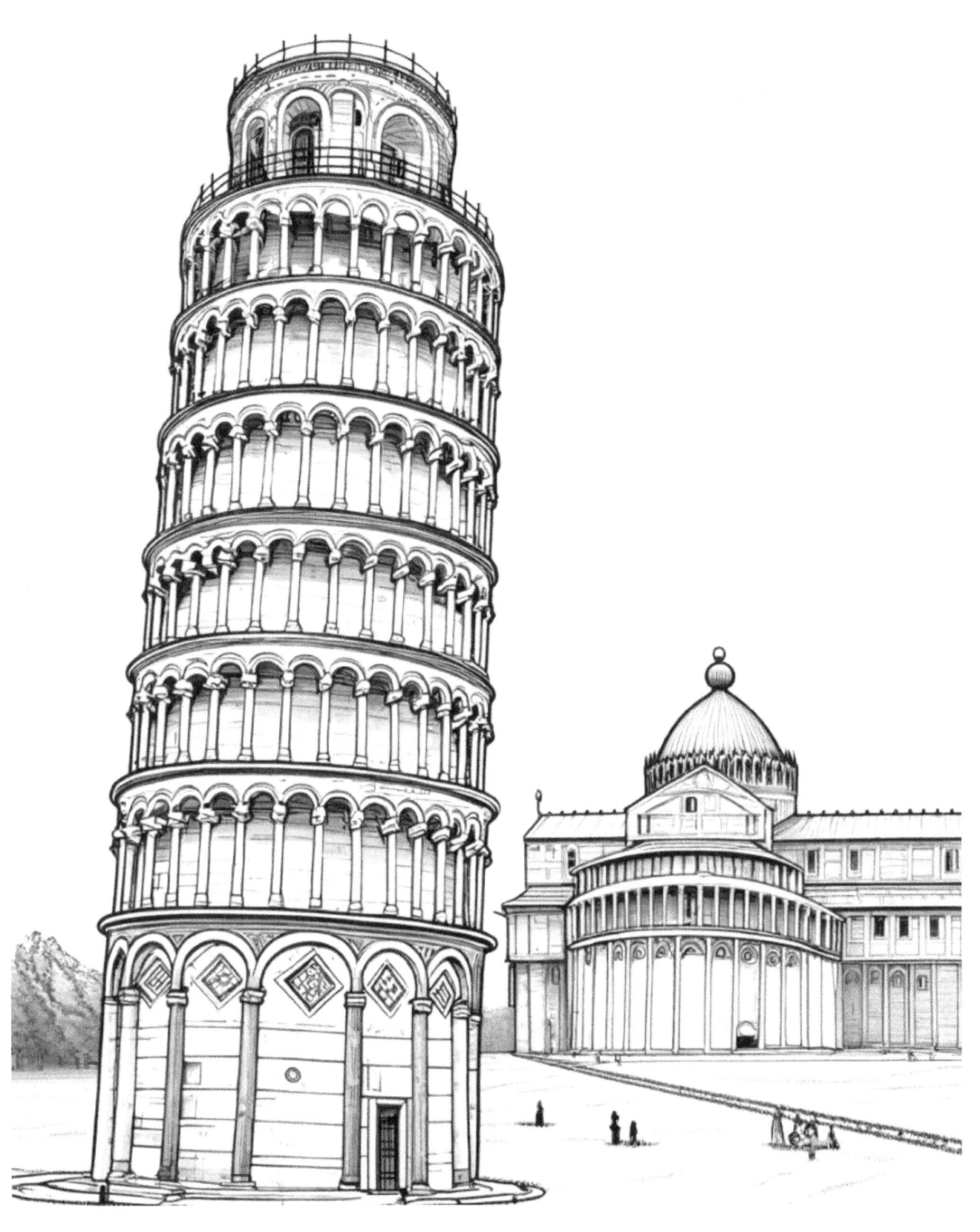

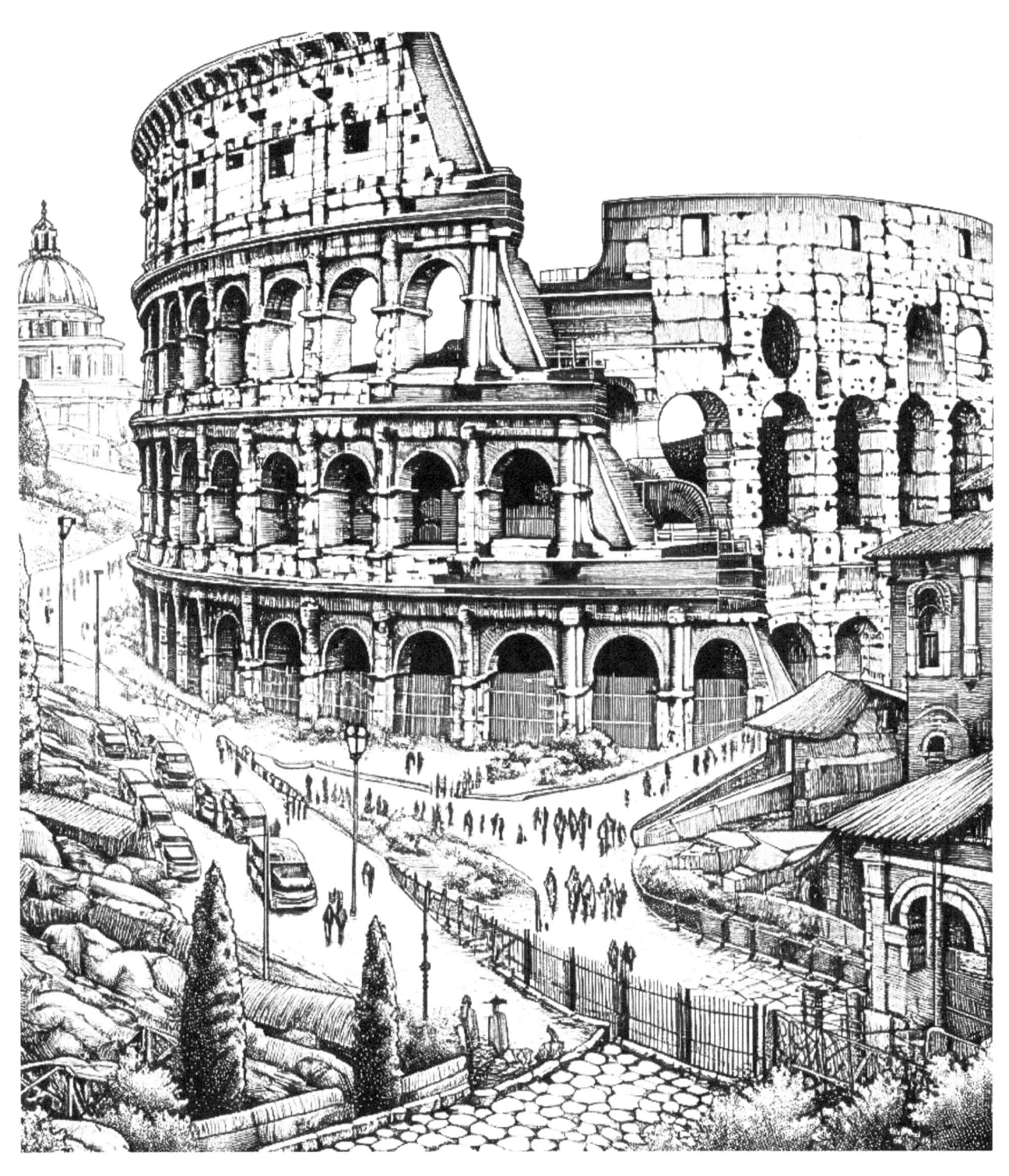

COLOSSEUM, ROME

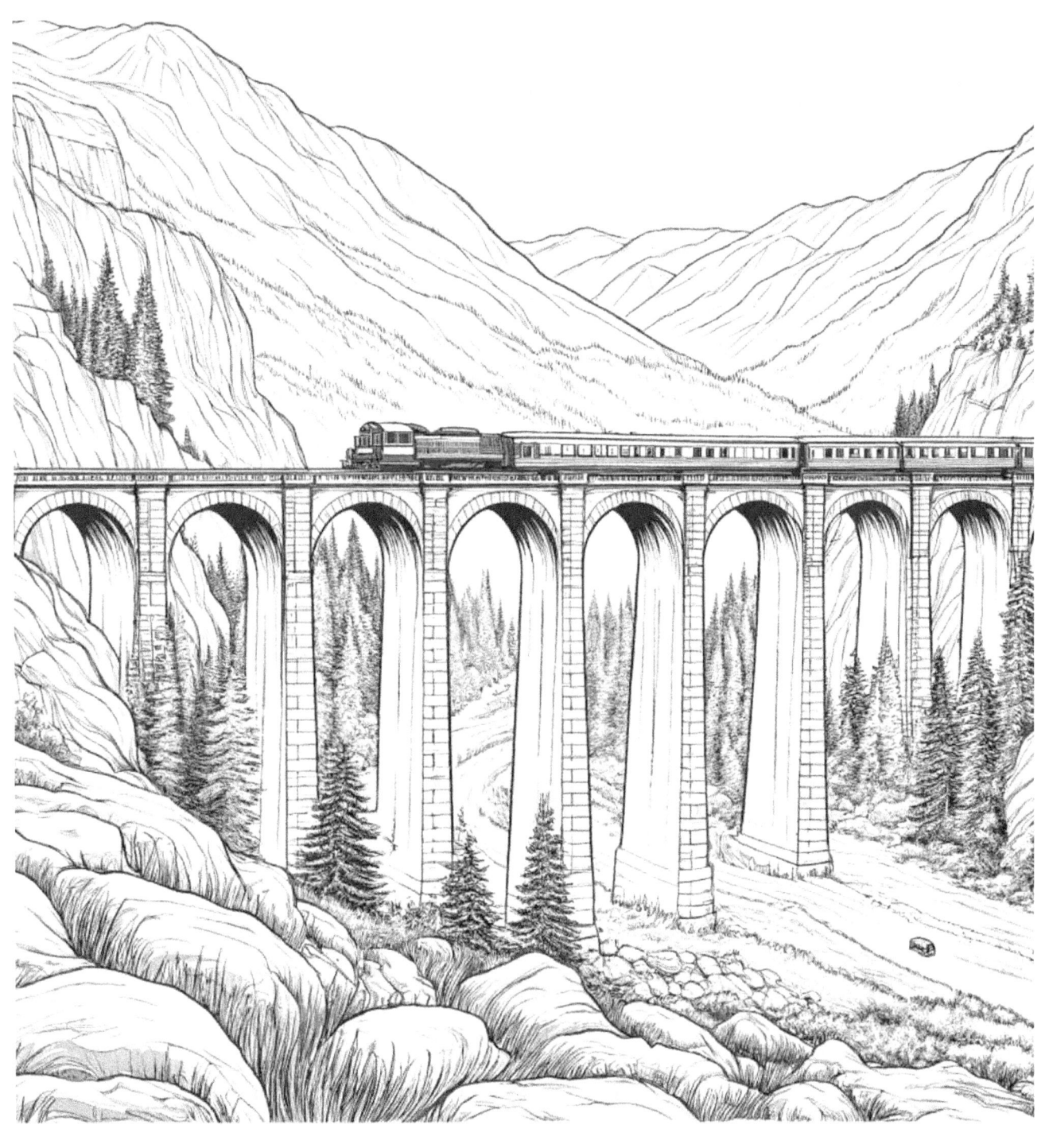

LANDWASSER
VIADUC.SWITZERLAND

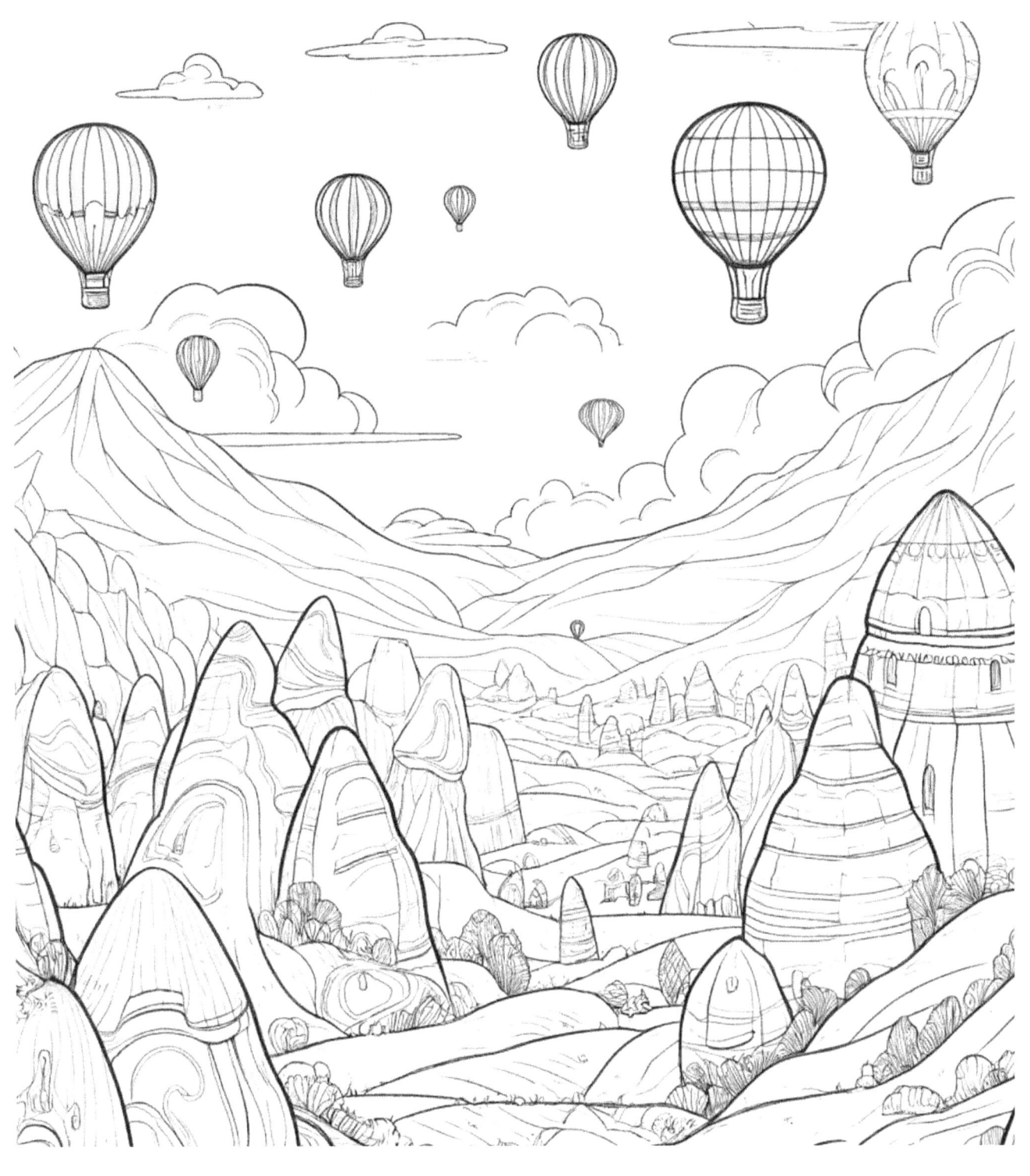

CAPPADOCIA.TURKEY

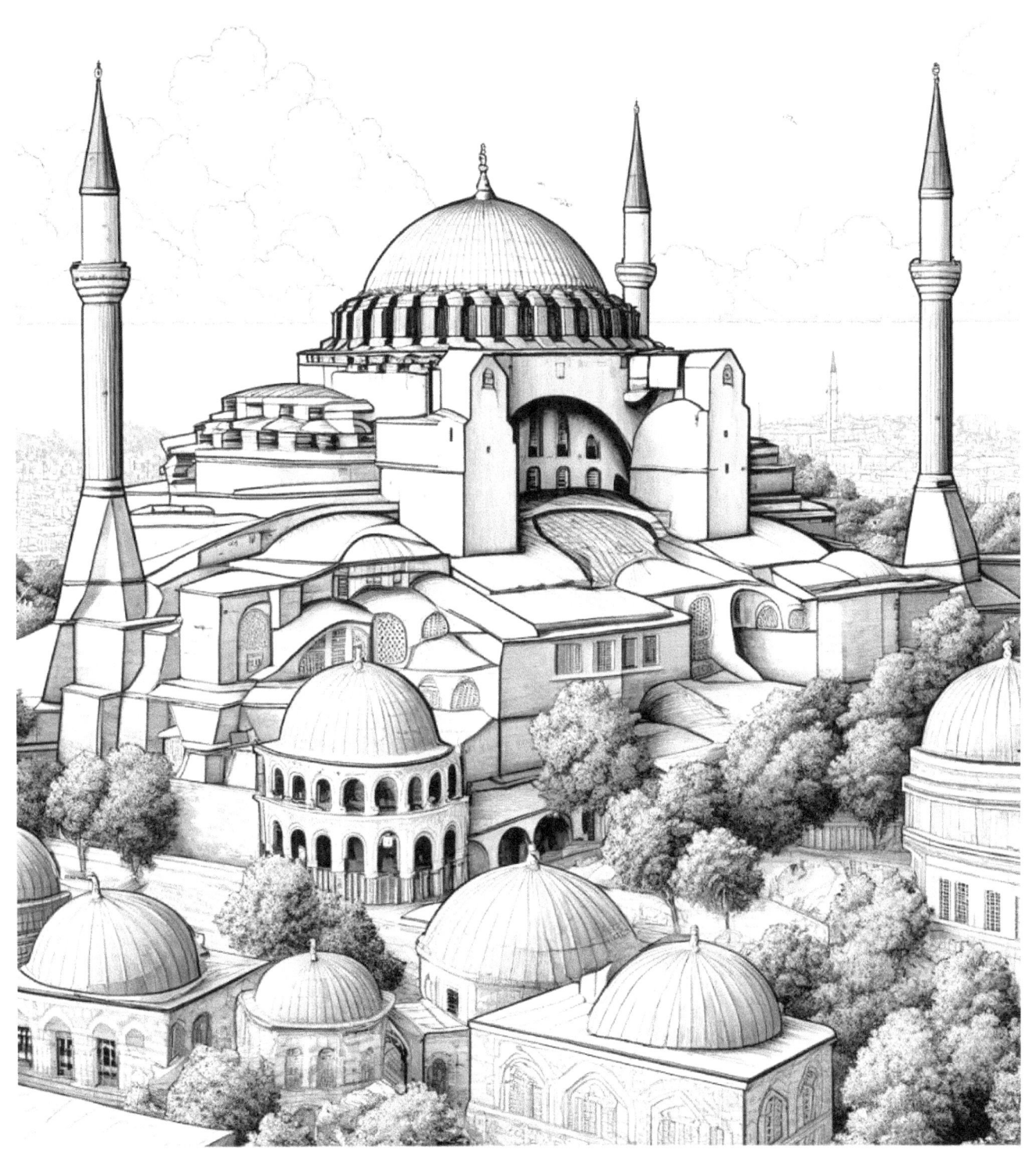

BLUE MOSQUE.ISTANBUL

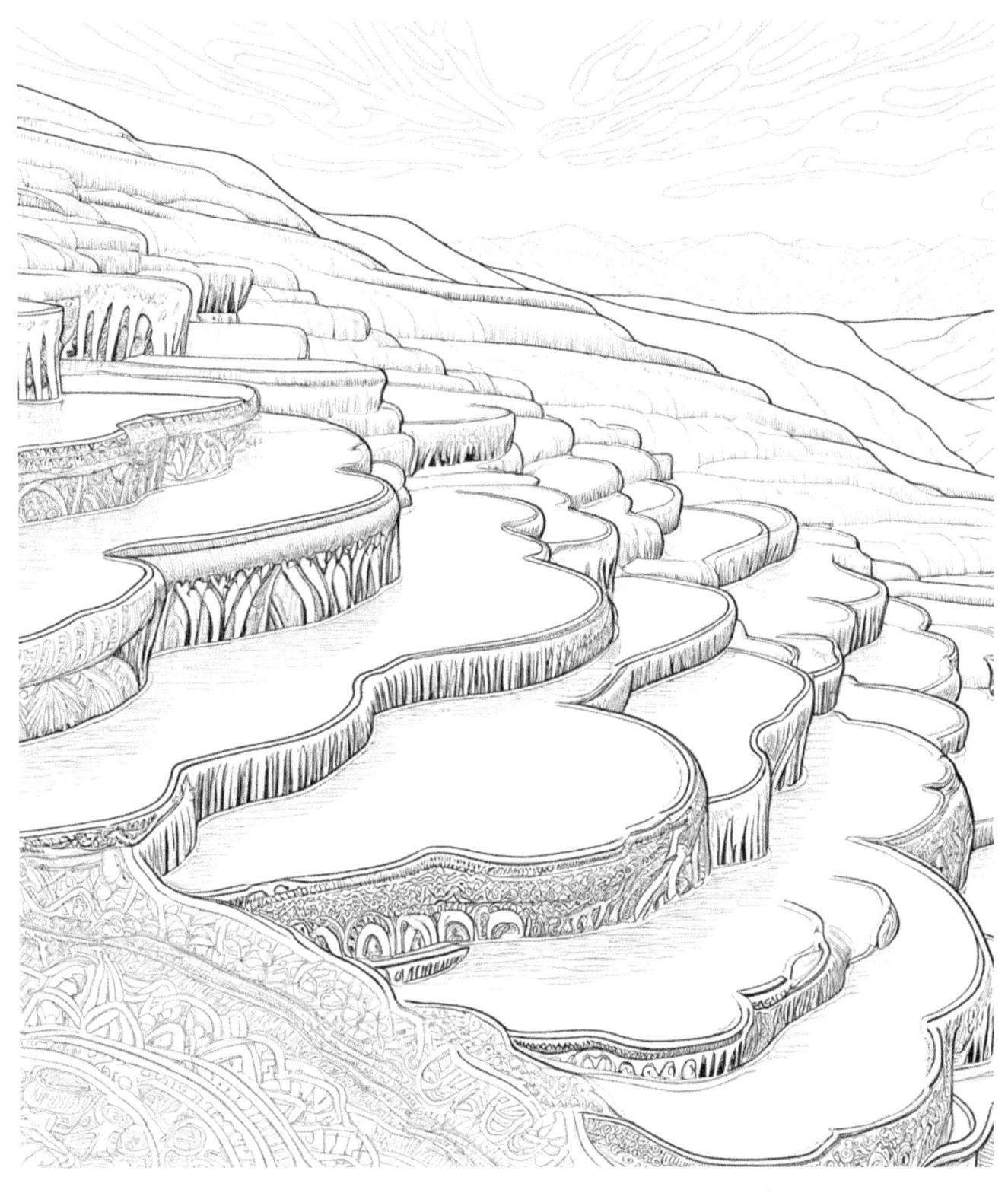

PAMUKKALE.TURKEY

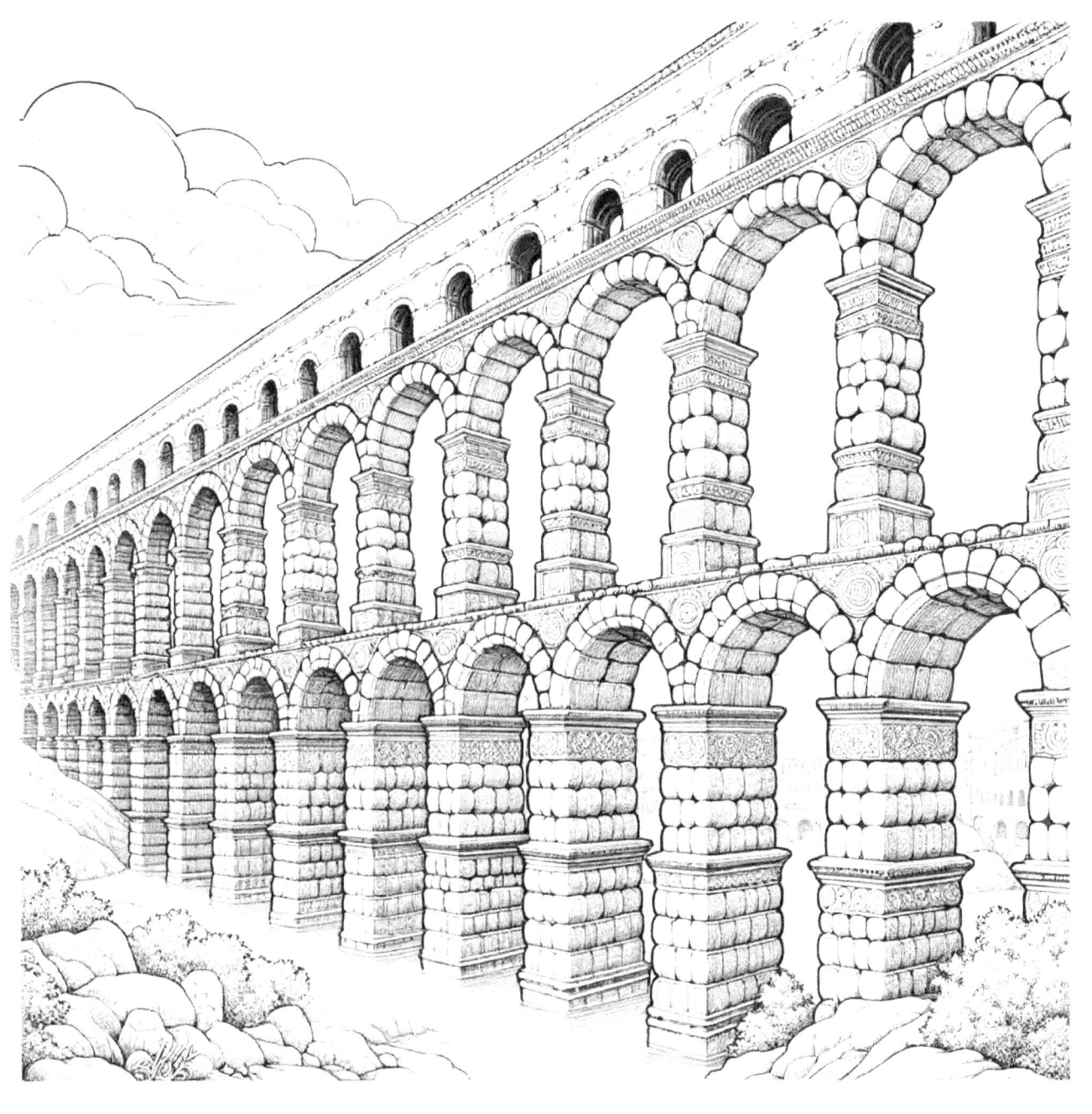

AQUEDUCT
ZAGHOUAN.TUNIS

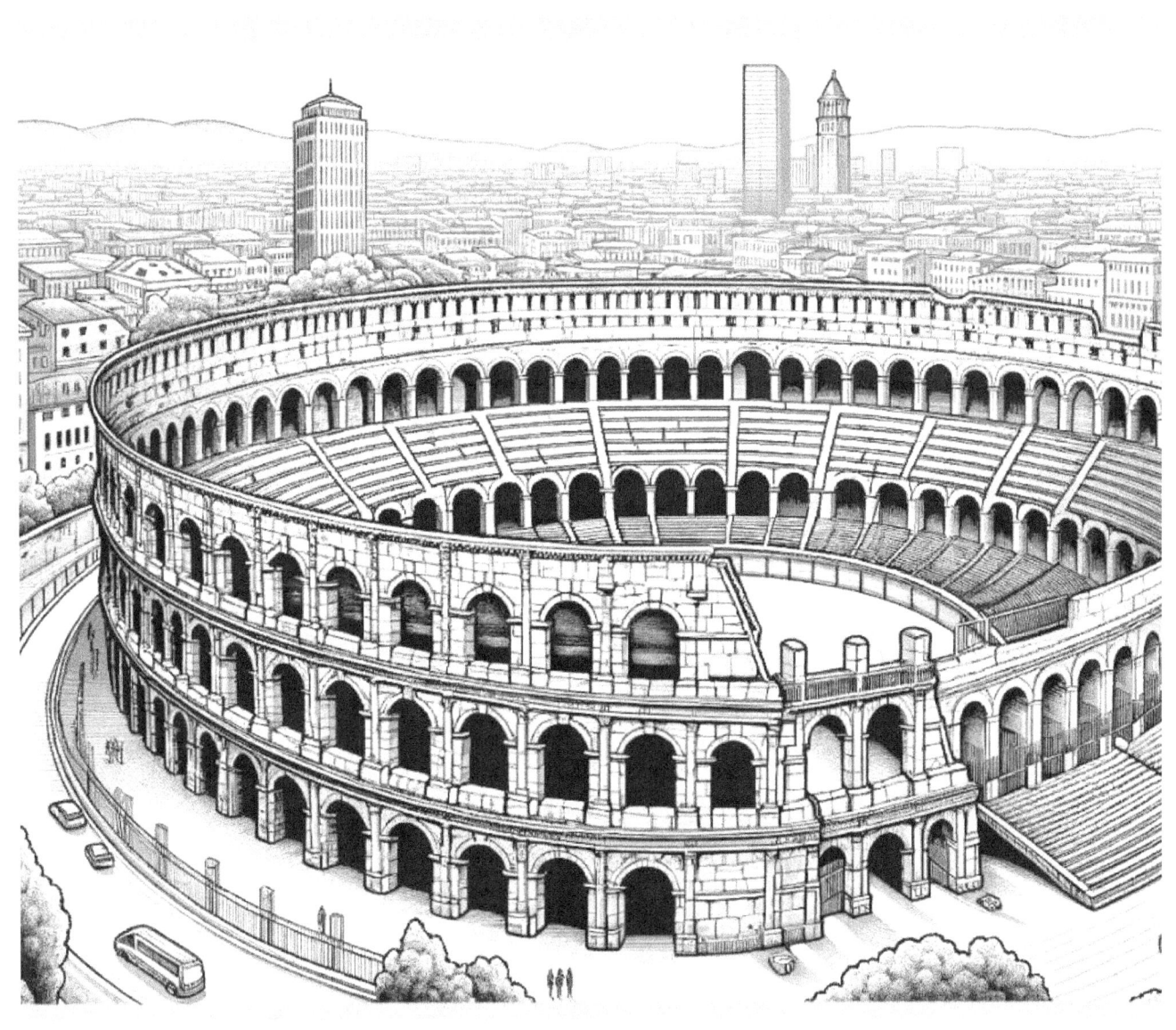

EL JEM
AMPHITHEATRE.TUNIS

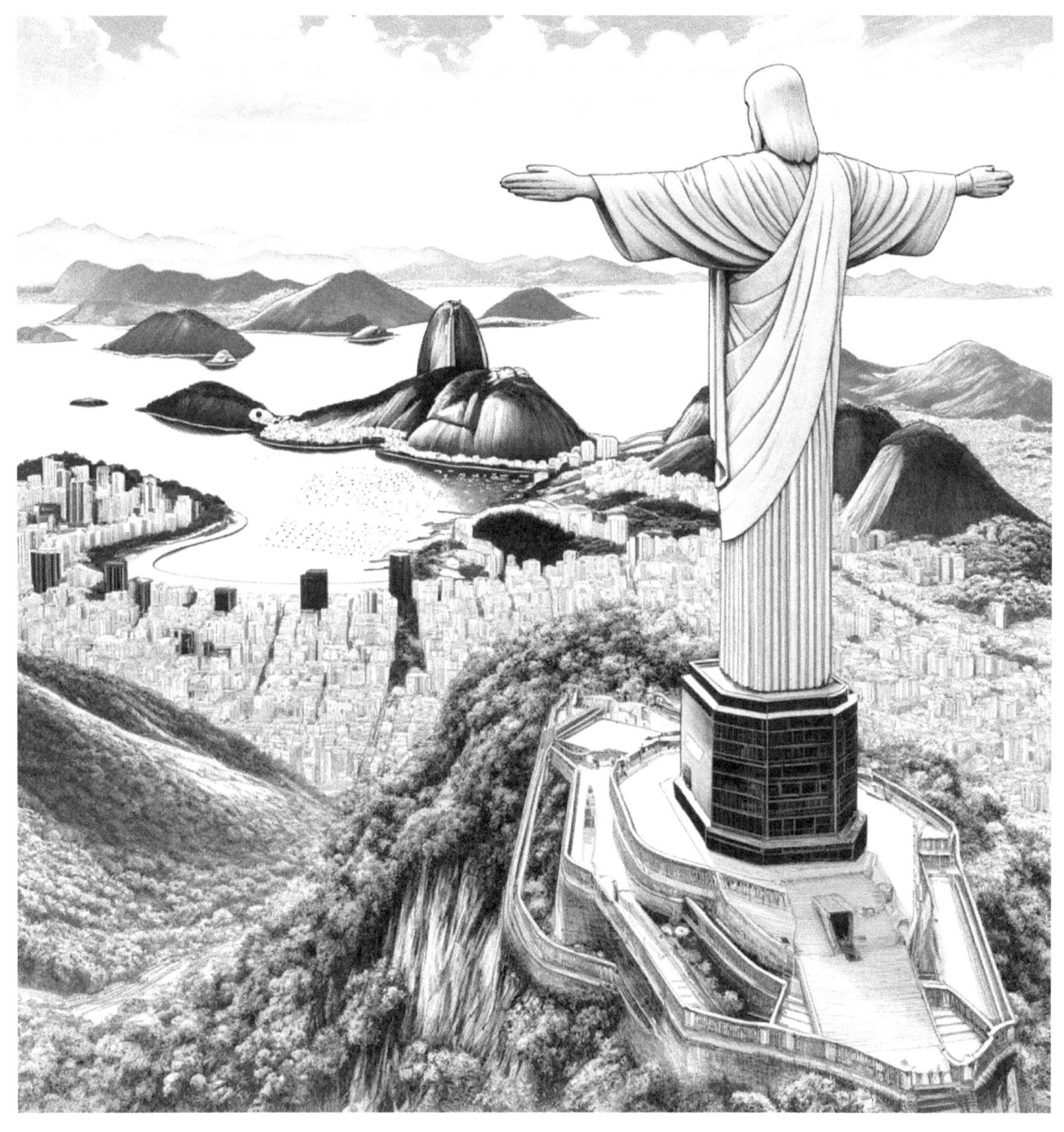

CHRIST THE REDEEMIER.BRASIL

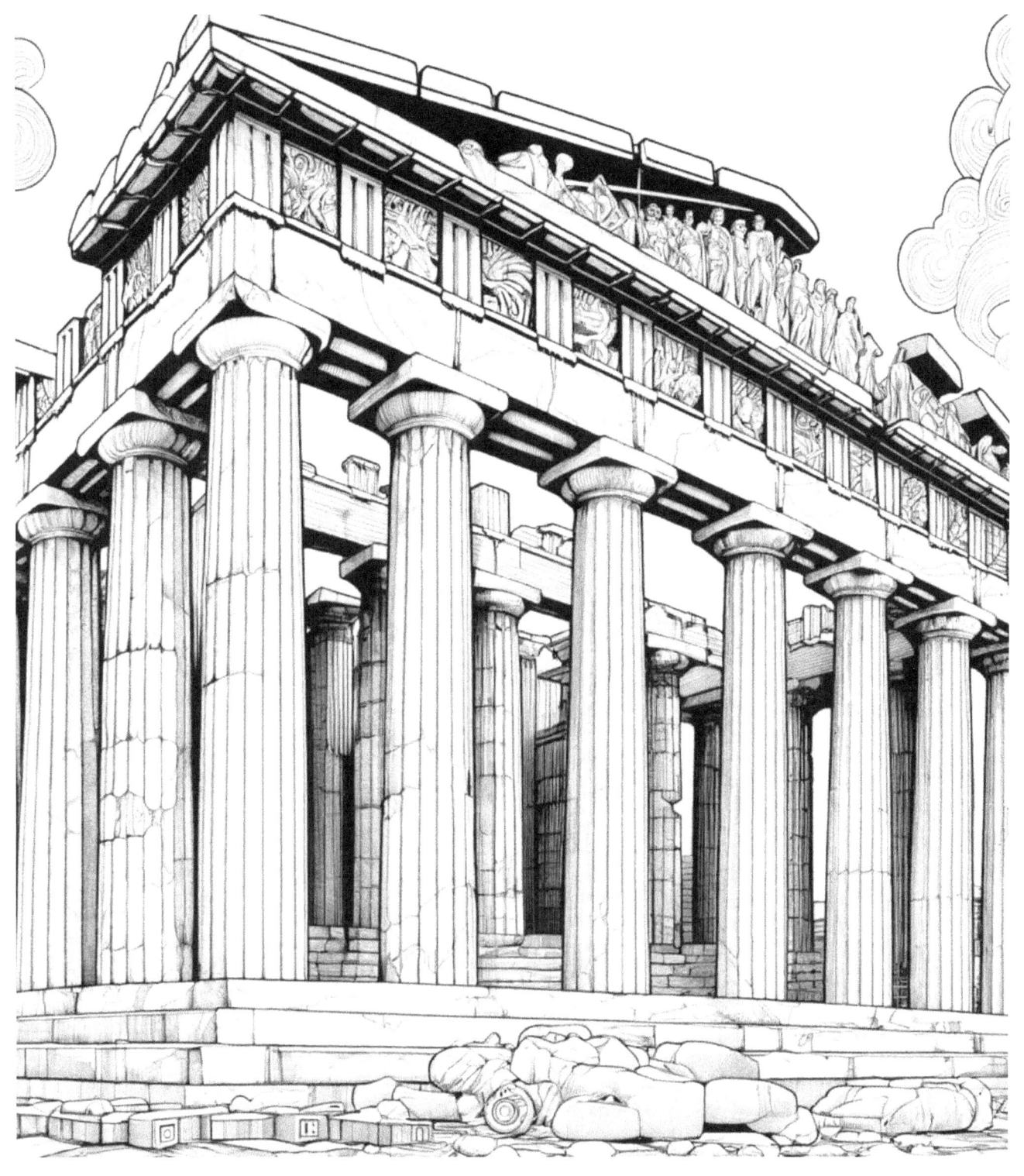

PARTHENON
ACROPOLE.GREECE

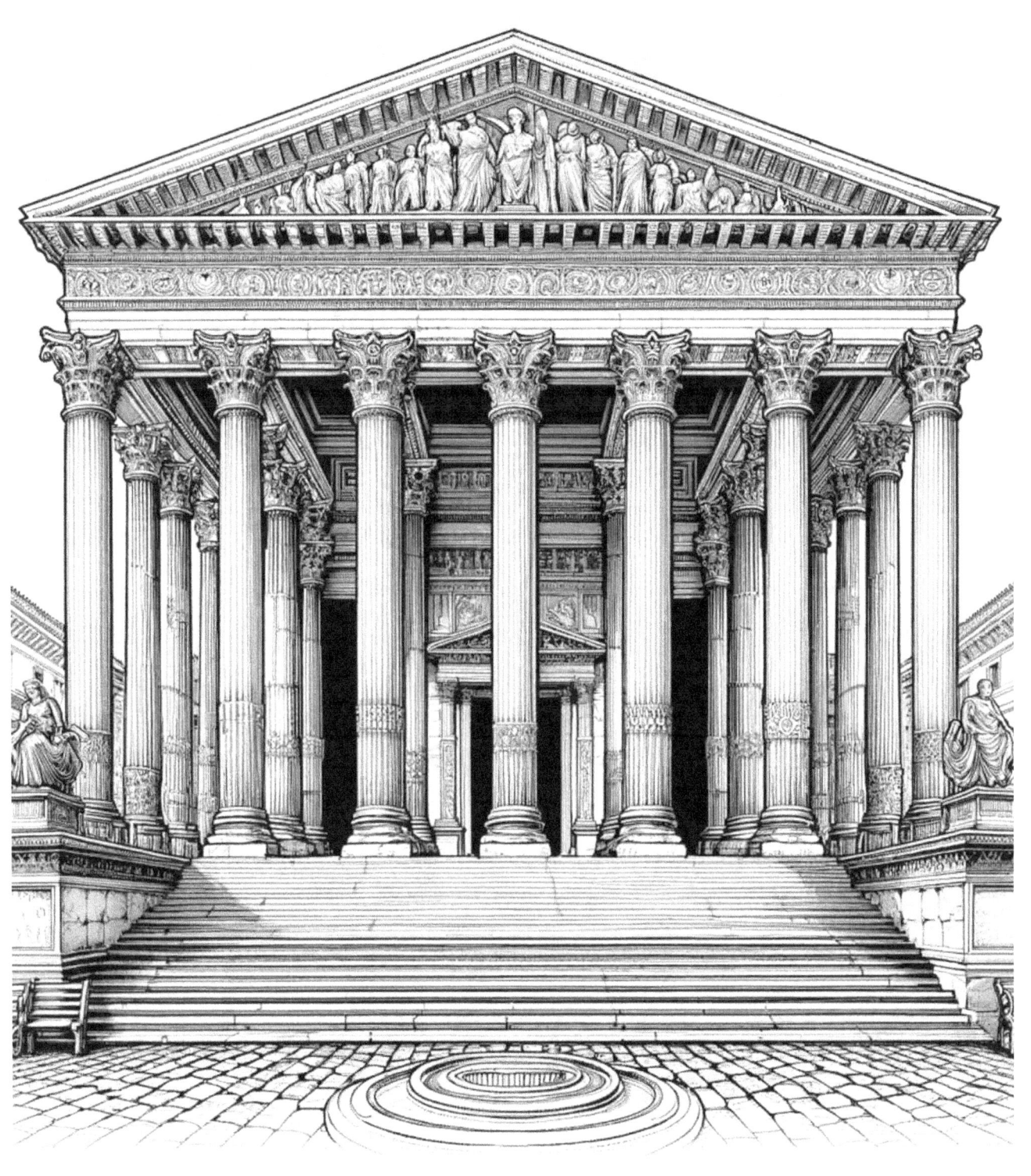

SQUARE HOUSE.FRANCE

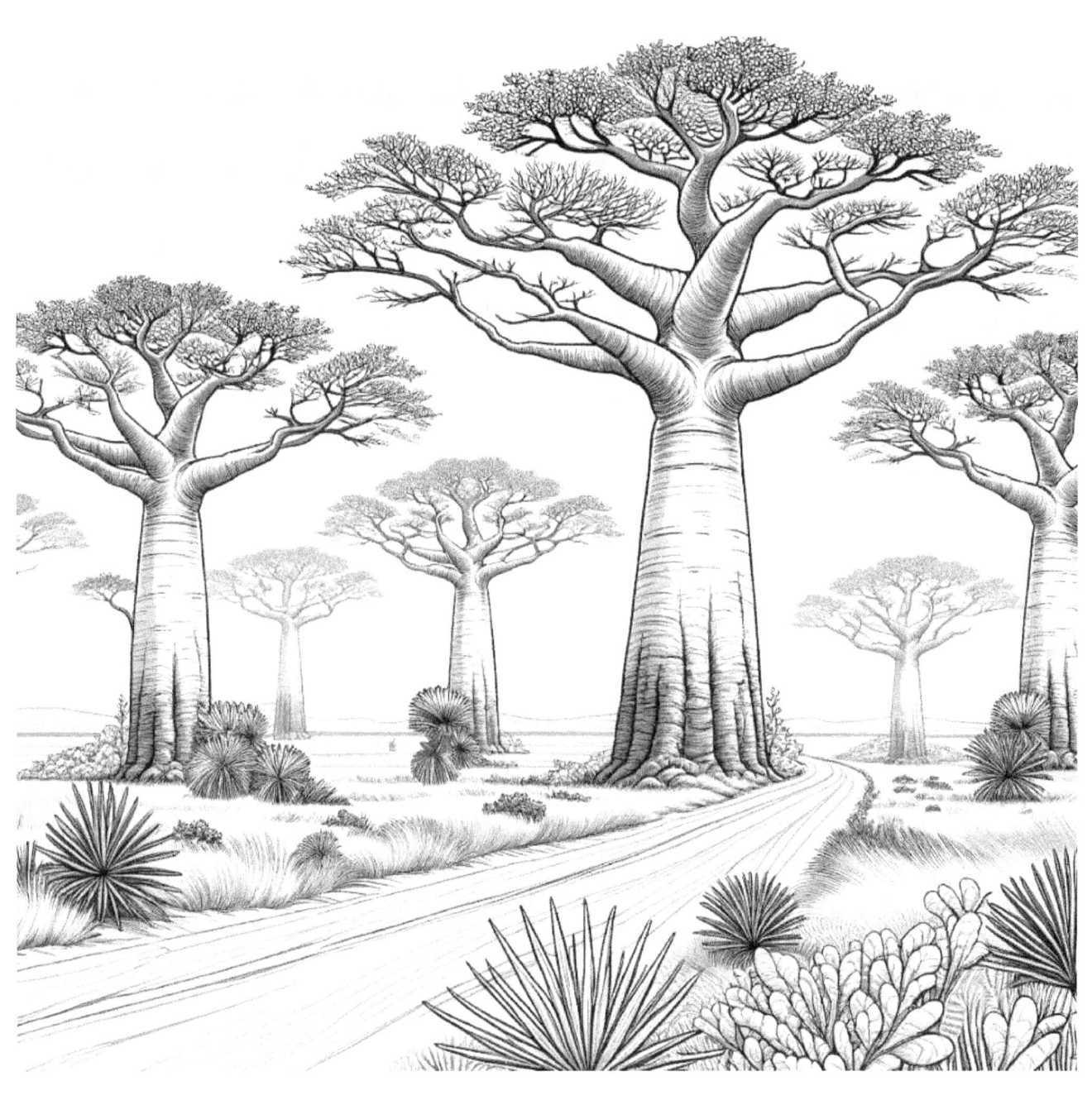

ALLEY OF
BAOBABS.MADAGASKAR

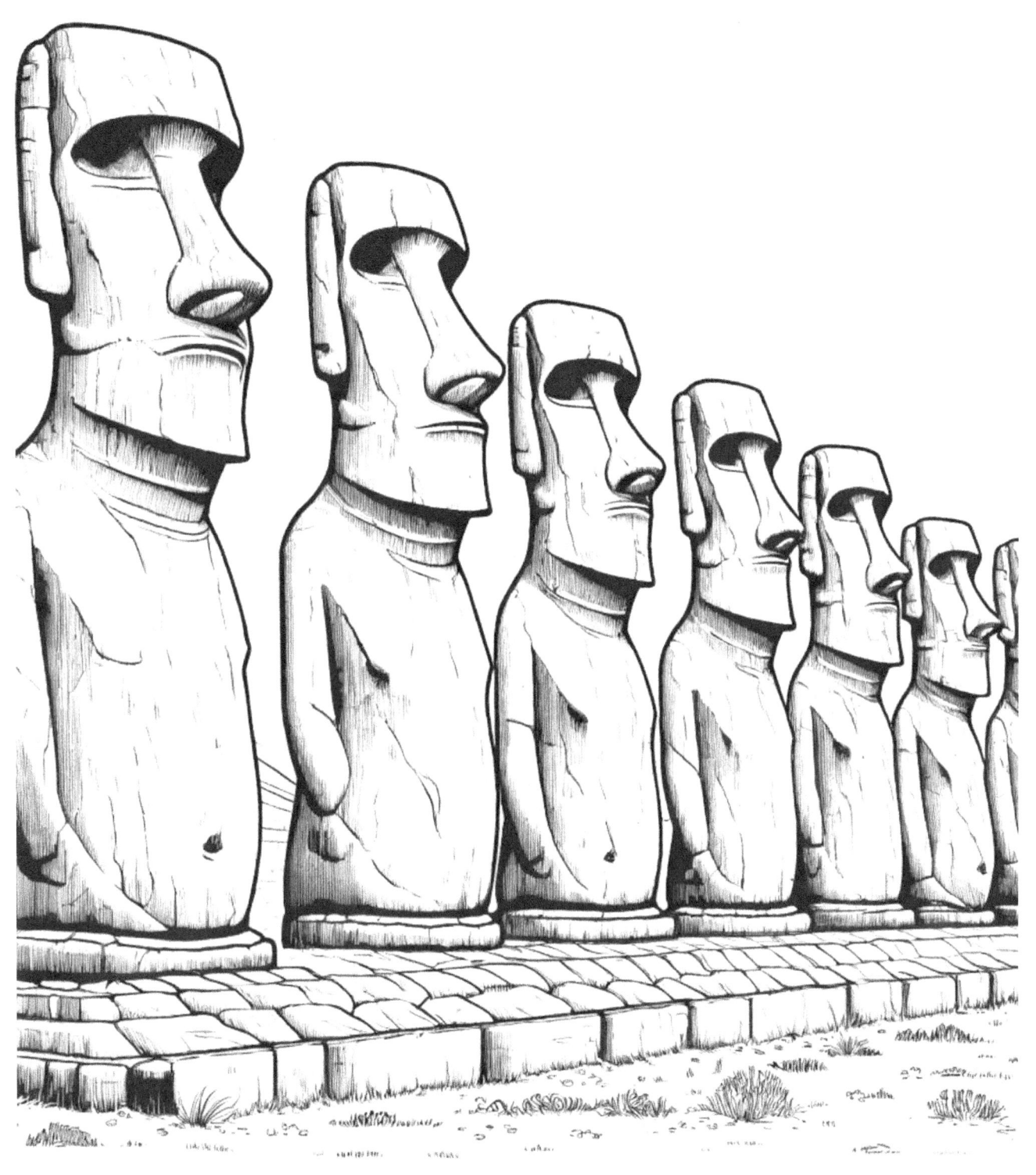

AHU TONGARIKI.CHILI

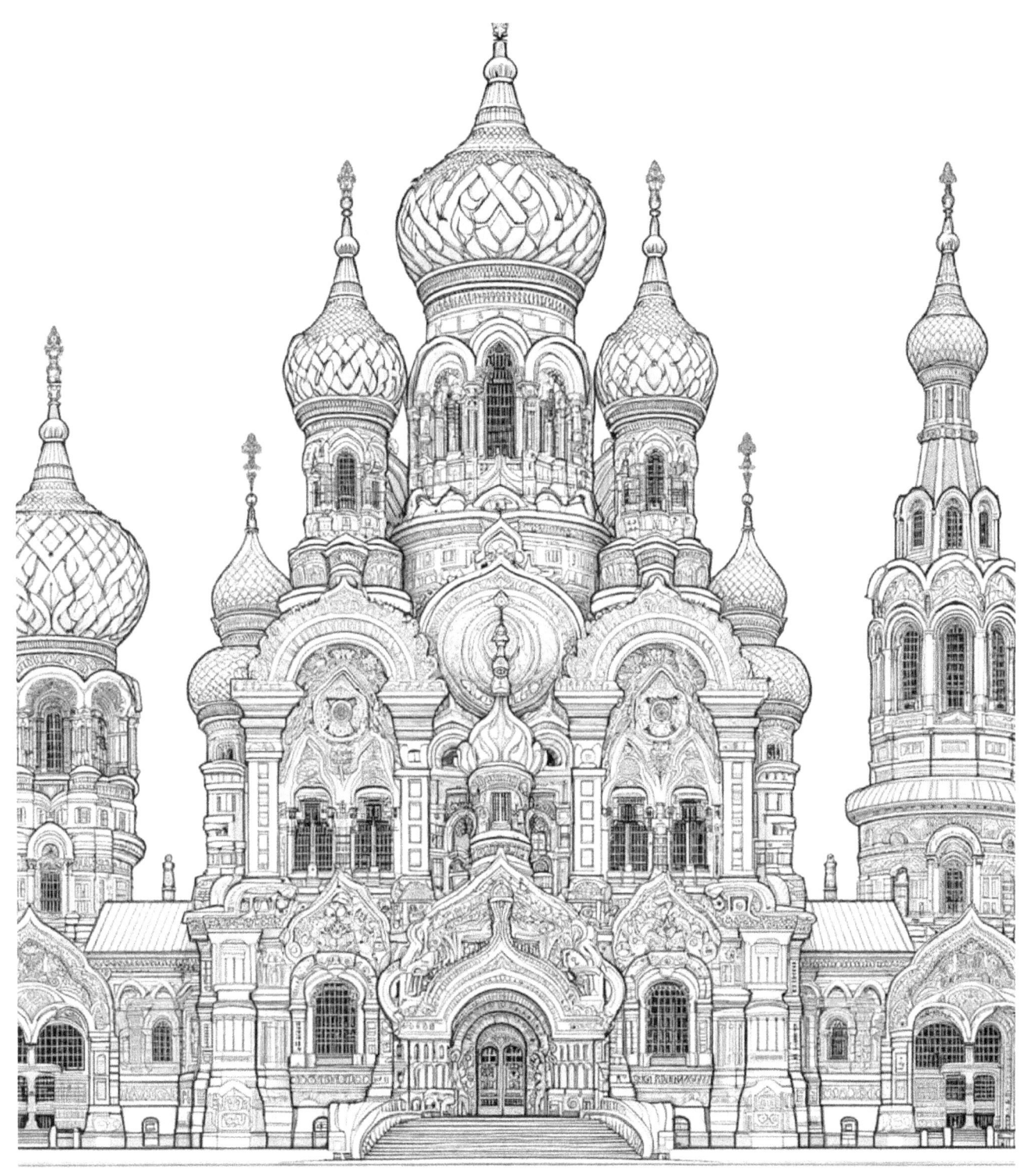

CATHEDRALE SAINT BASIL.MOSCOW

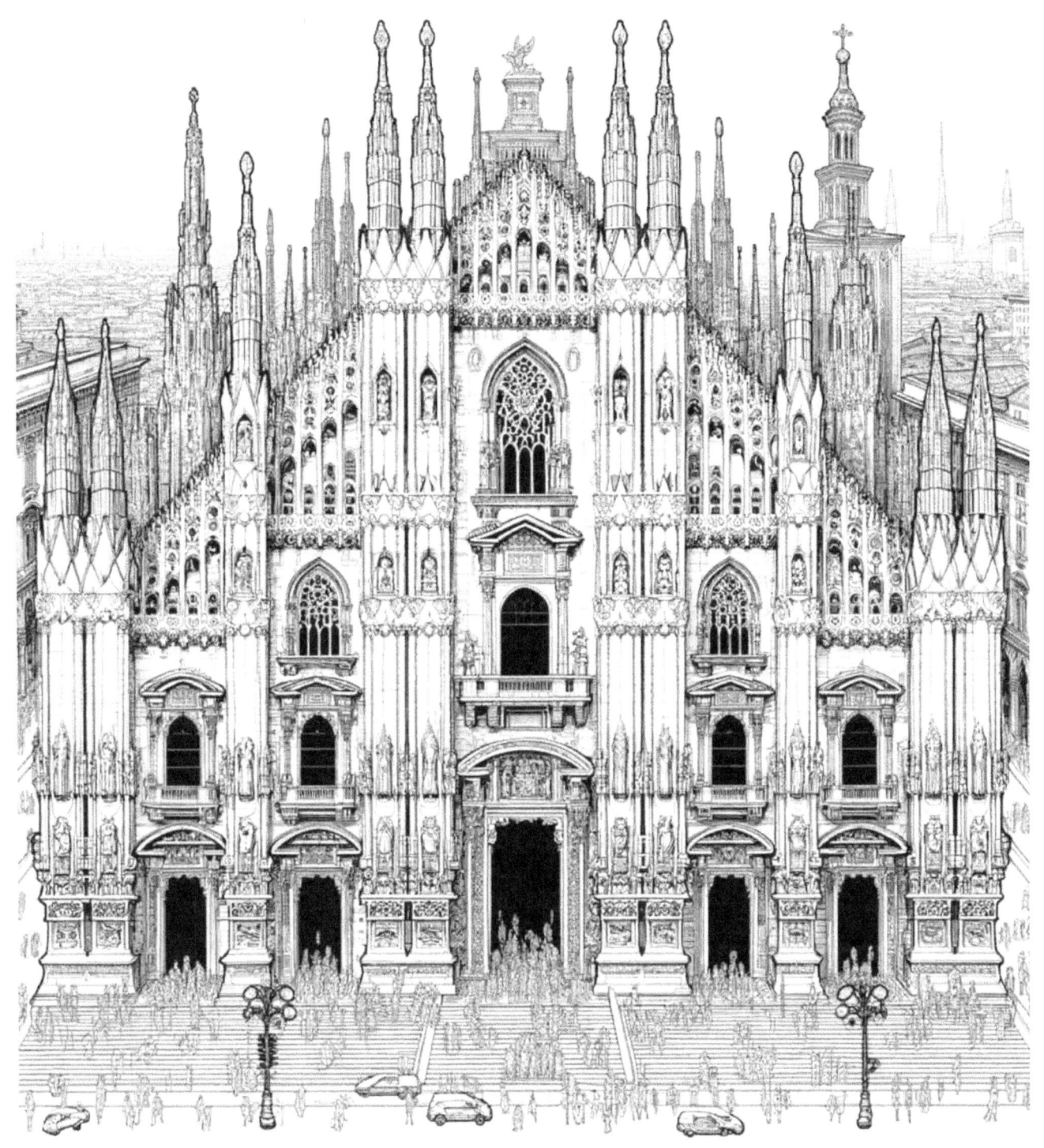

MILAN
CATHEDRAL.ITALIA

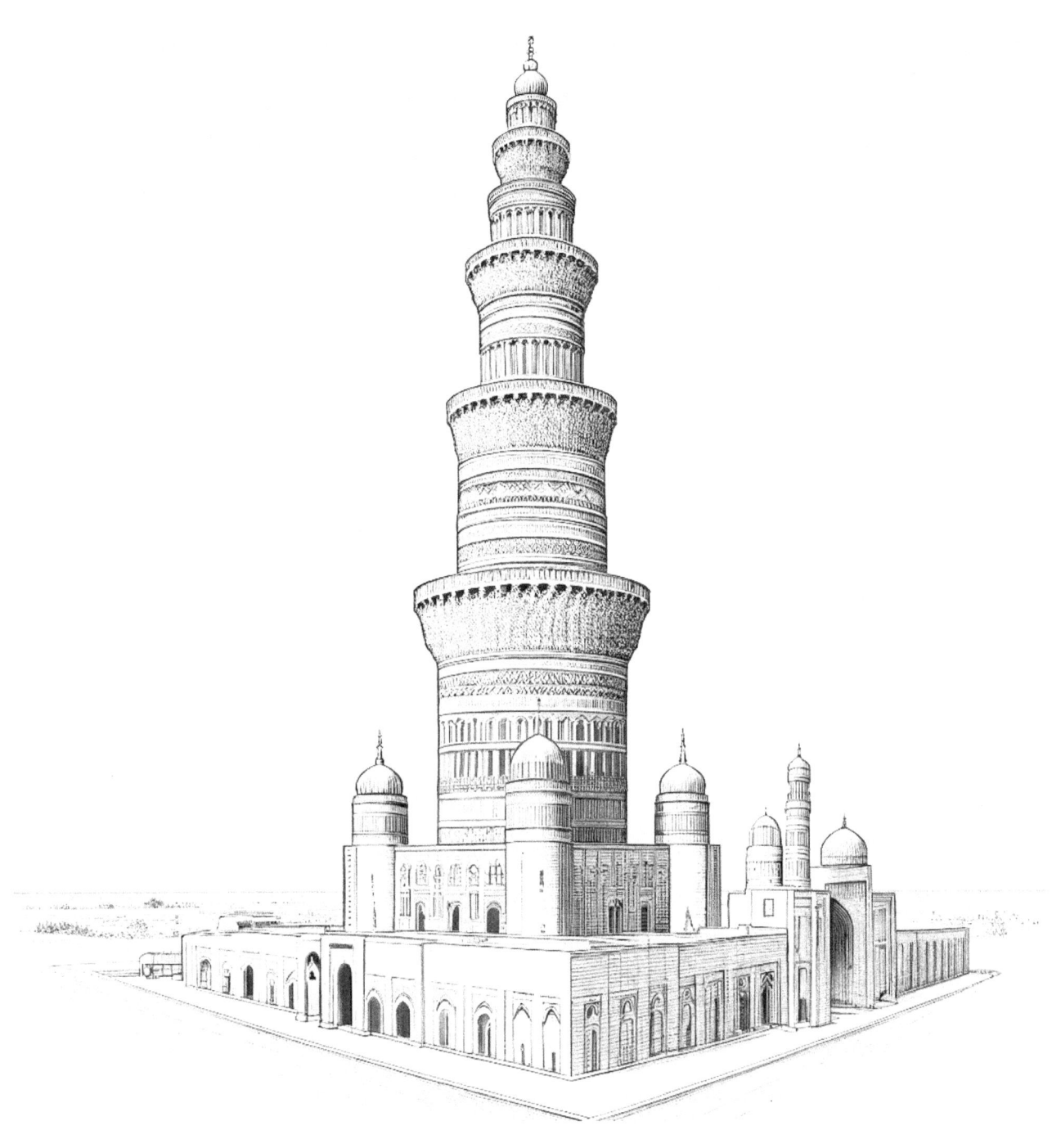

THE GREAT MOSQUE OF SAMARRA, IRAQ

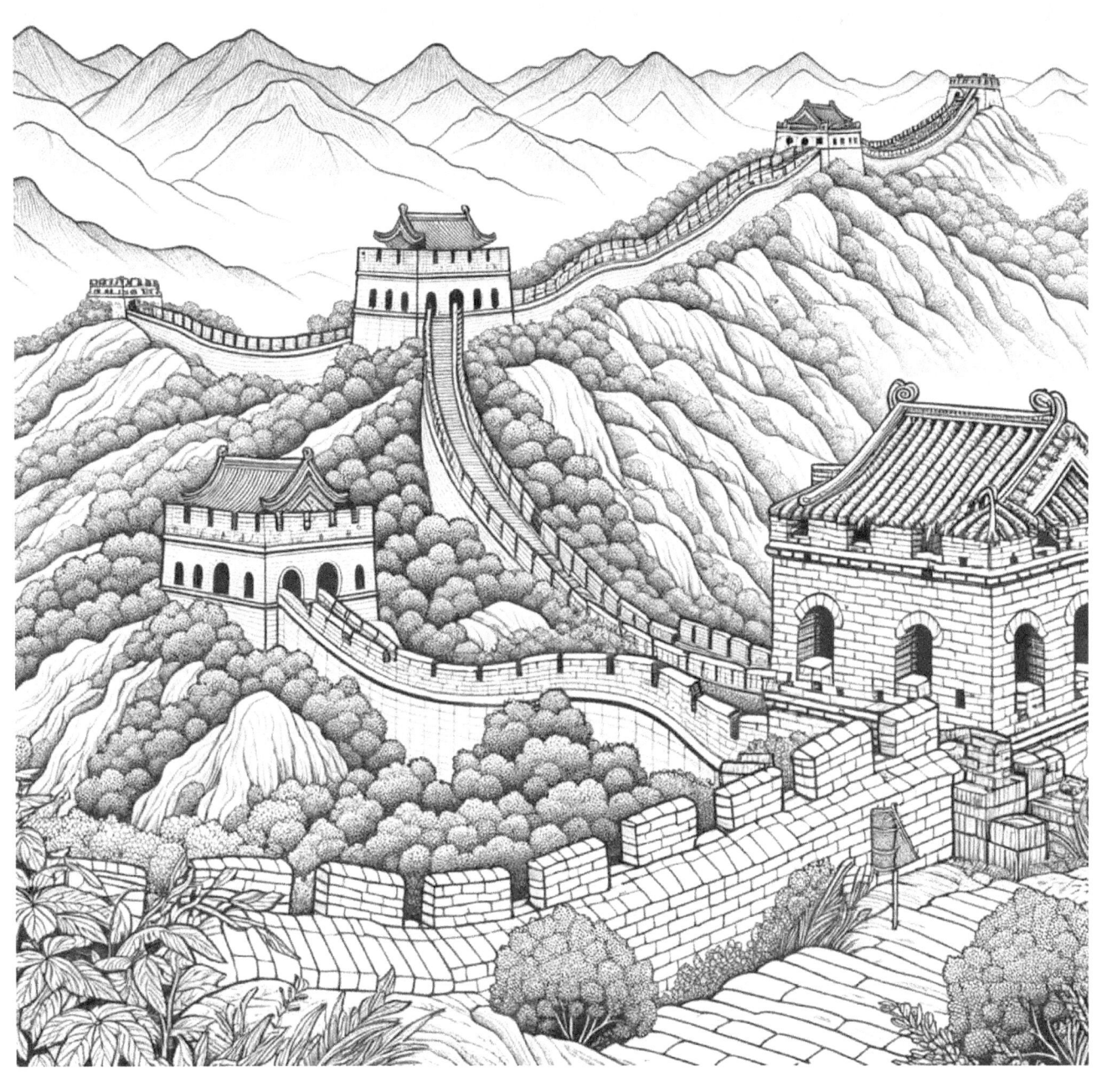

THE GREAT WALL.CHINA

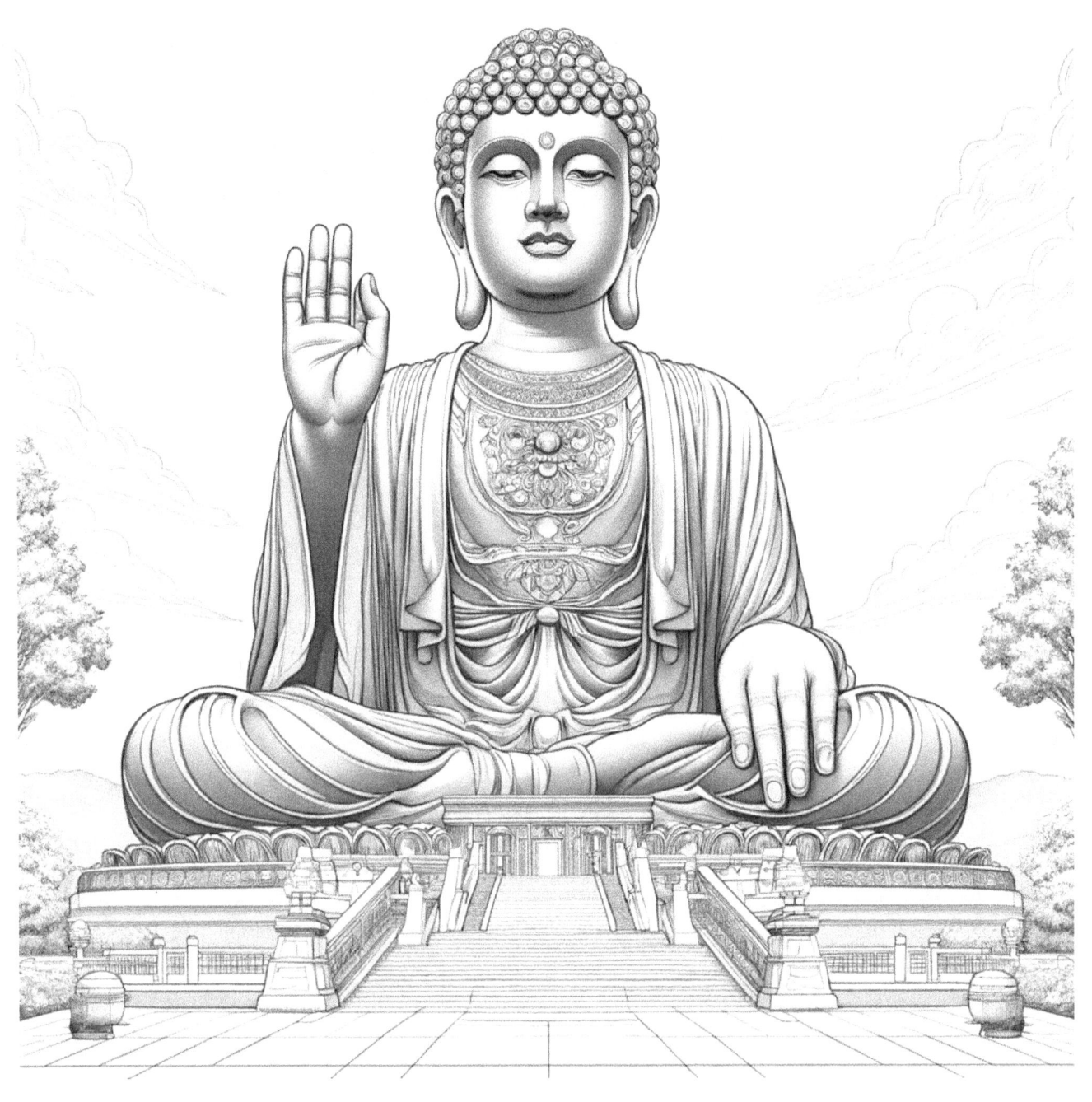

SOURCE TEMPLE
BUDDHA.CHINA

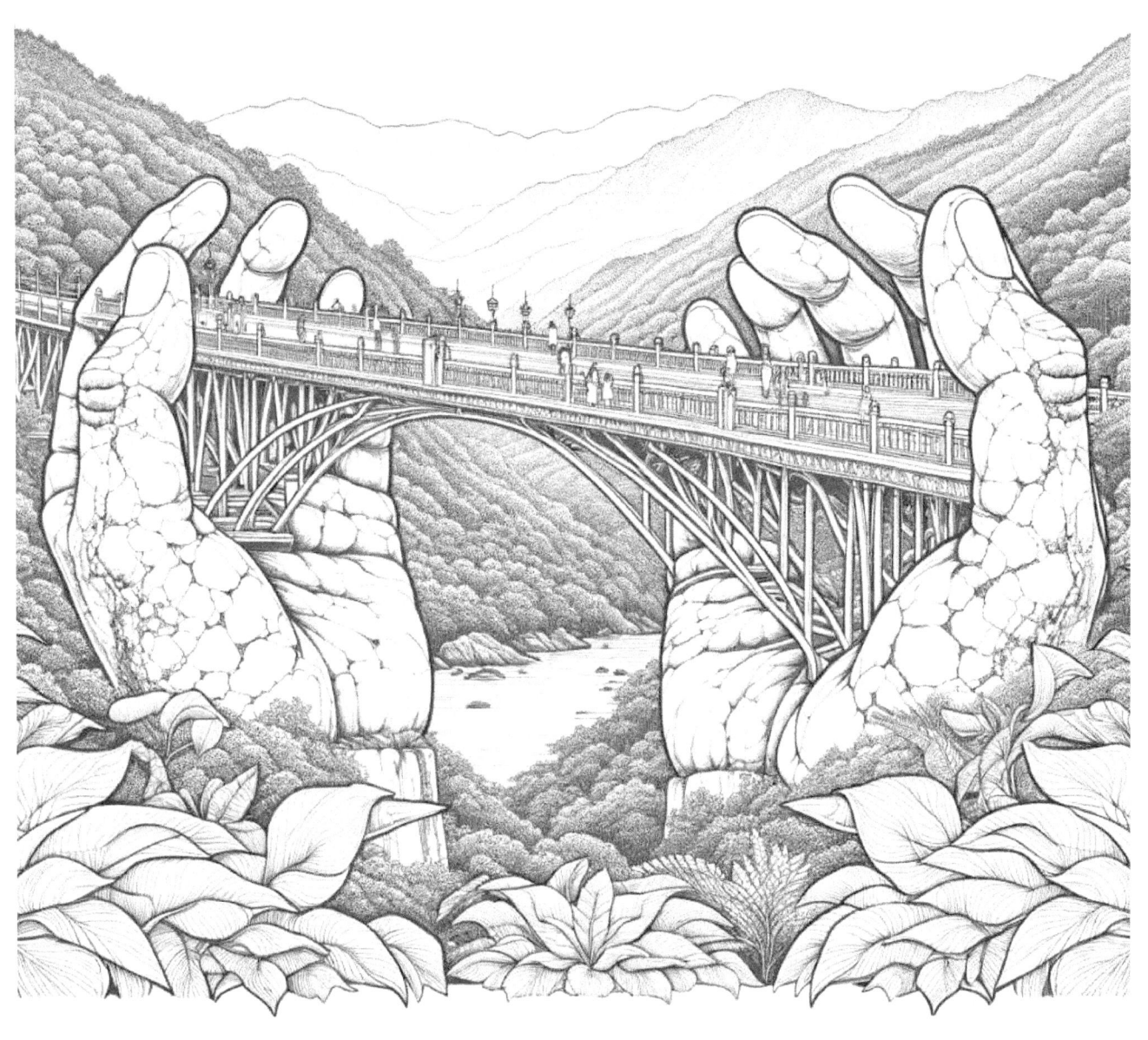

BA NA HILLS.VIETNAM

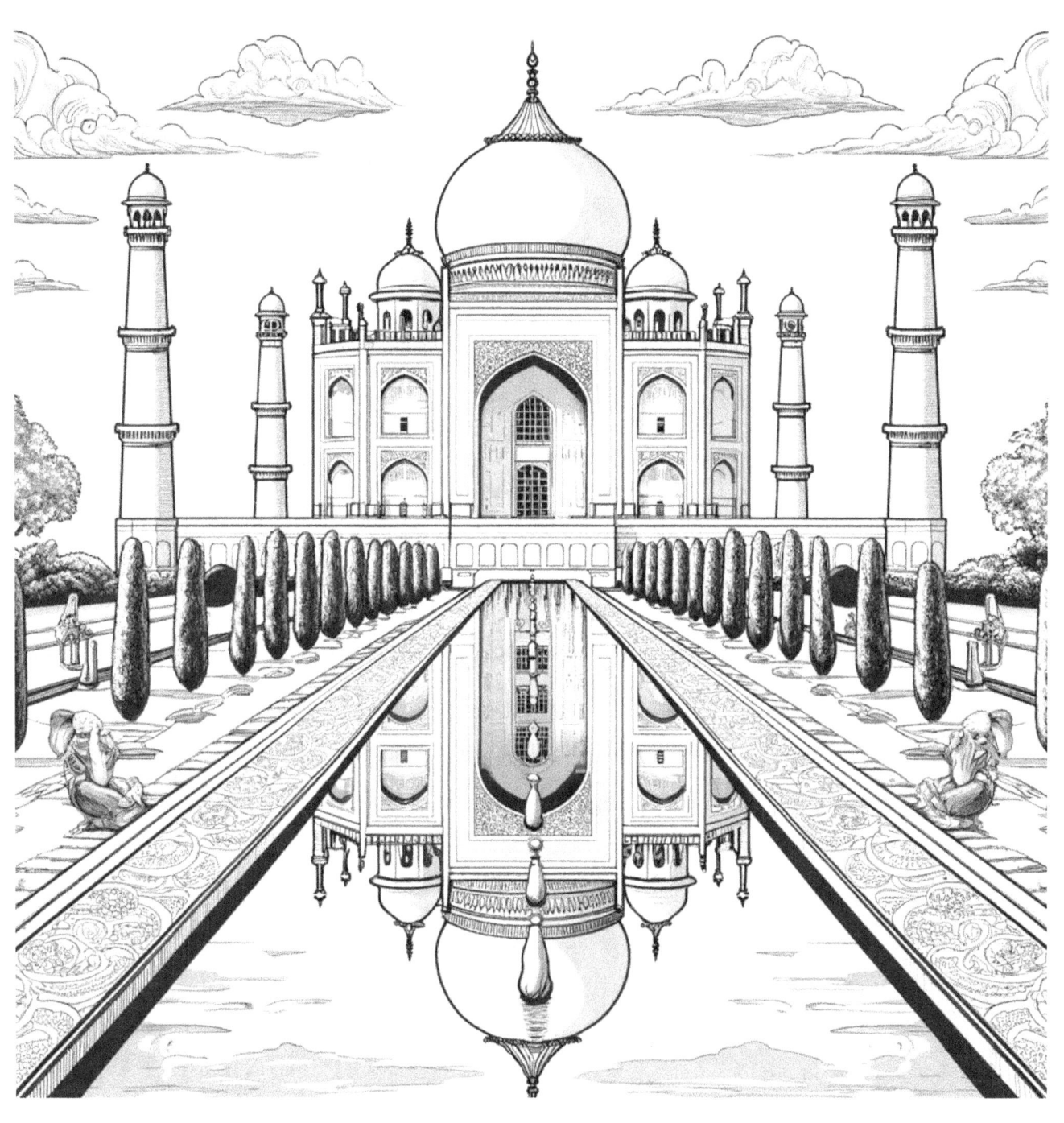

TAJ MAHAL.INDIA

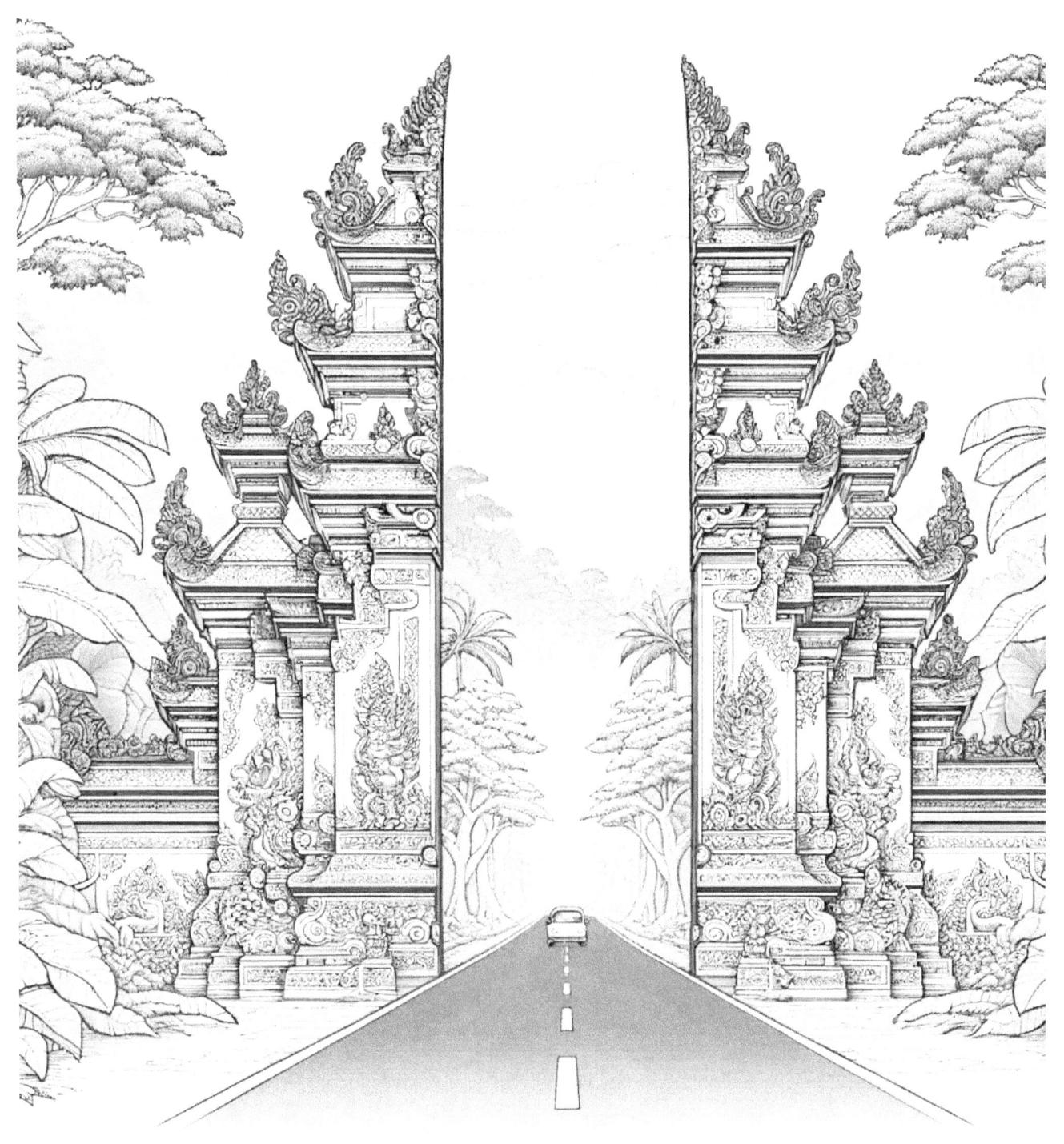

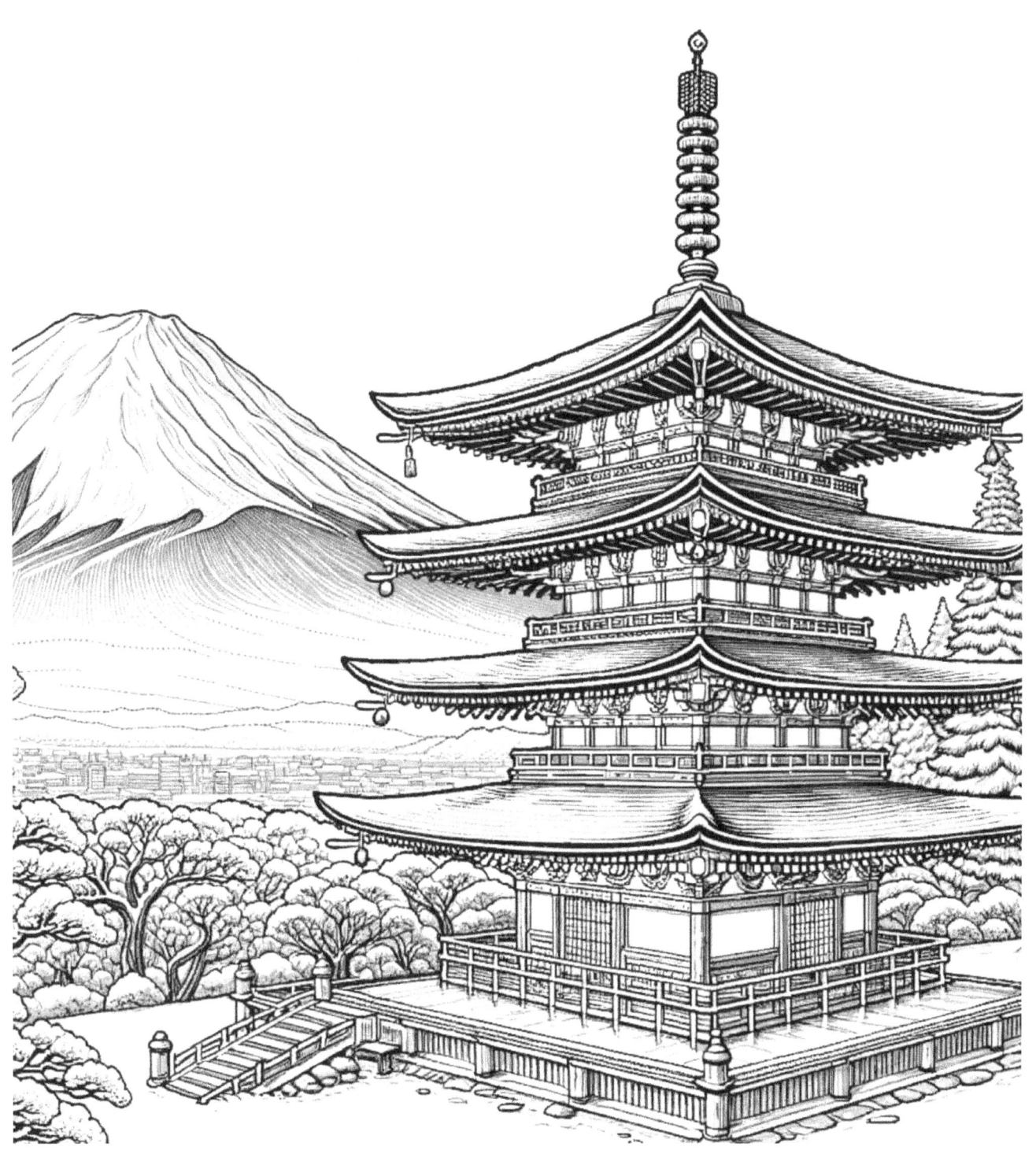

FUJI MOUNTAIN.JAPAN

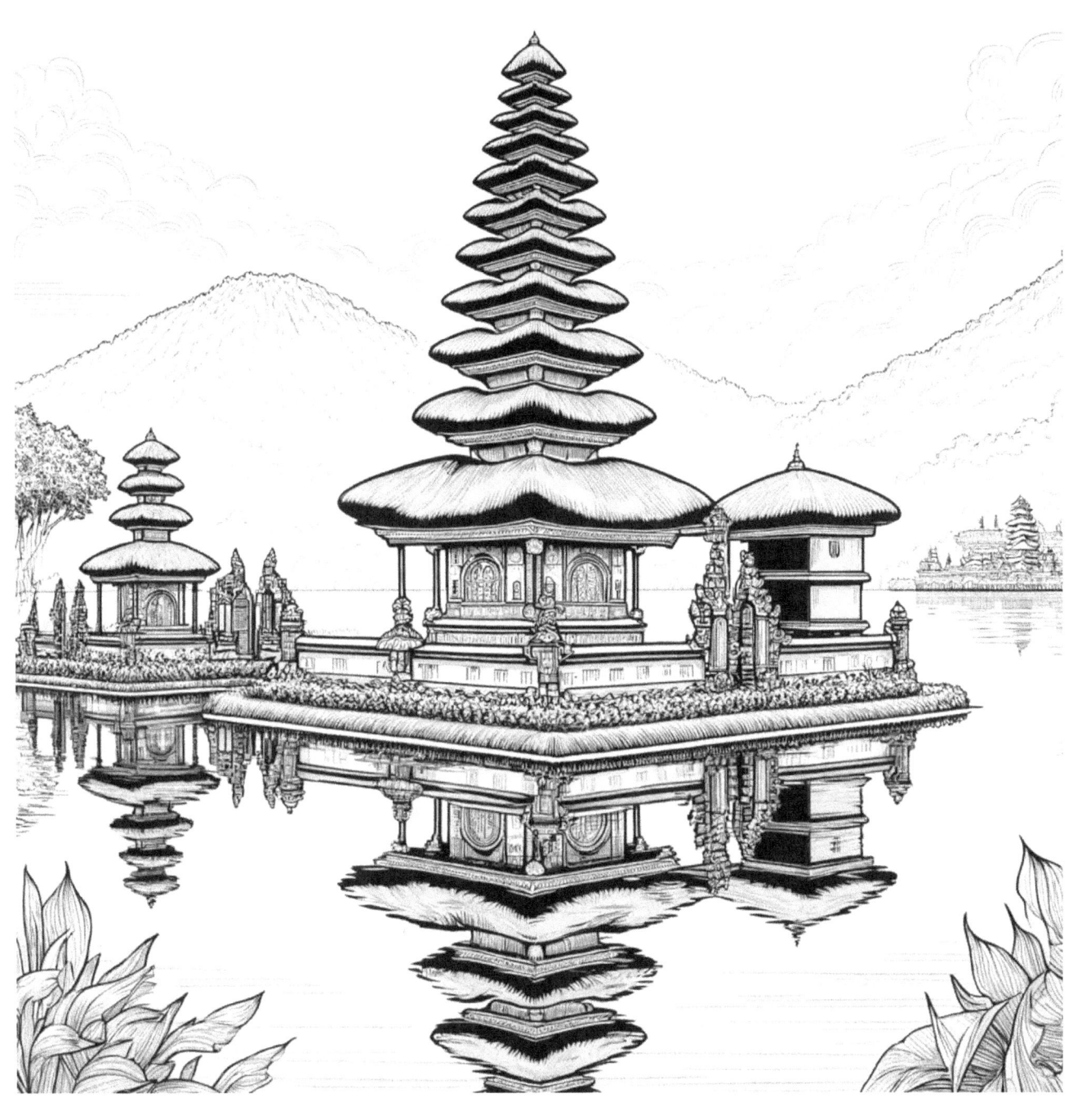

LAKE BRATAN.BALI

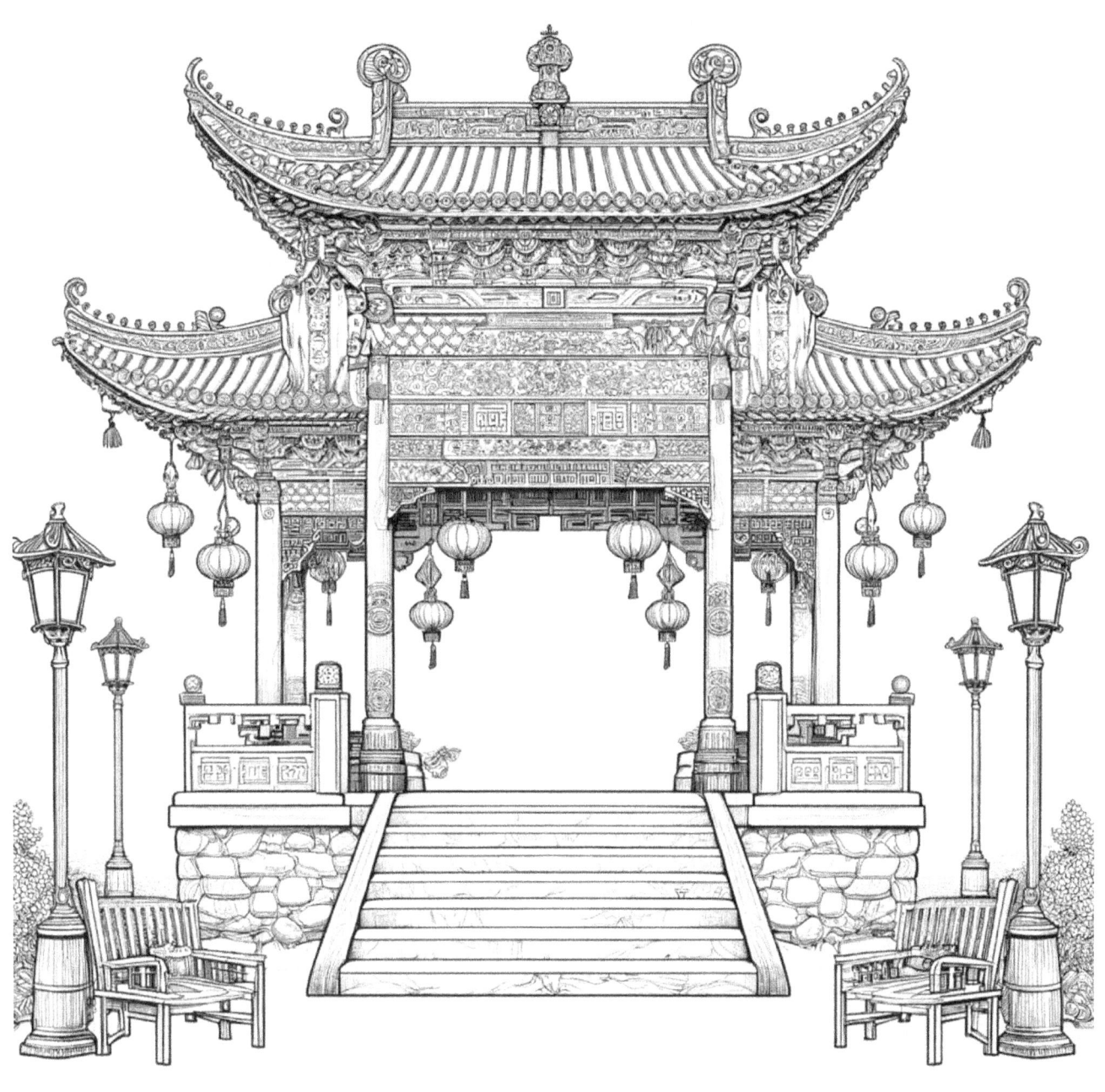

DRAGON DESCENDANTS MUSEUM.THAILAND

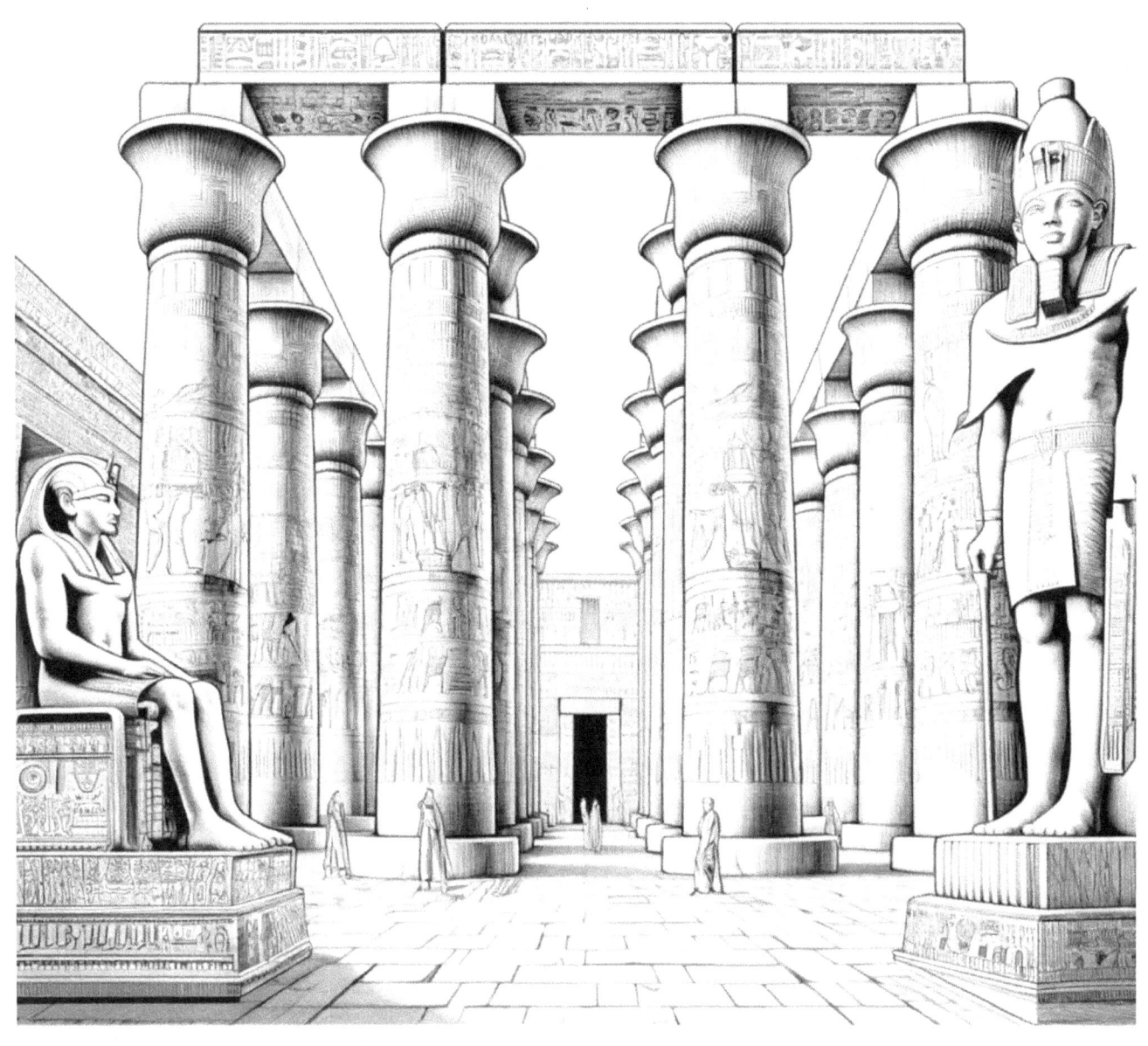

KARNAK TEMPLE.EGYPT

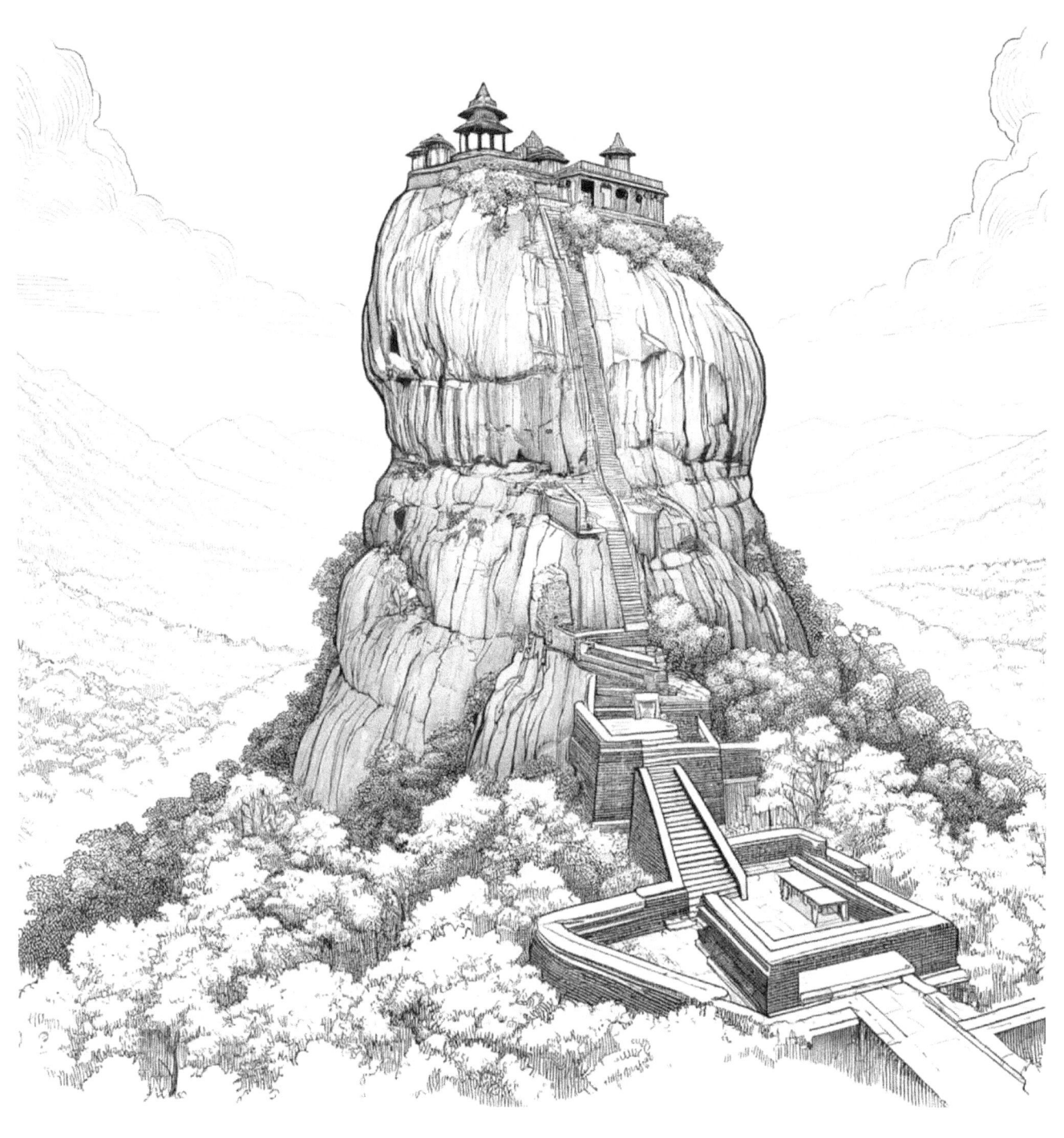

SIGIRIYA.SRI LANKA

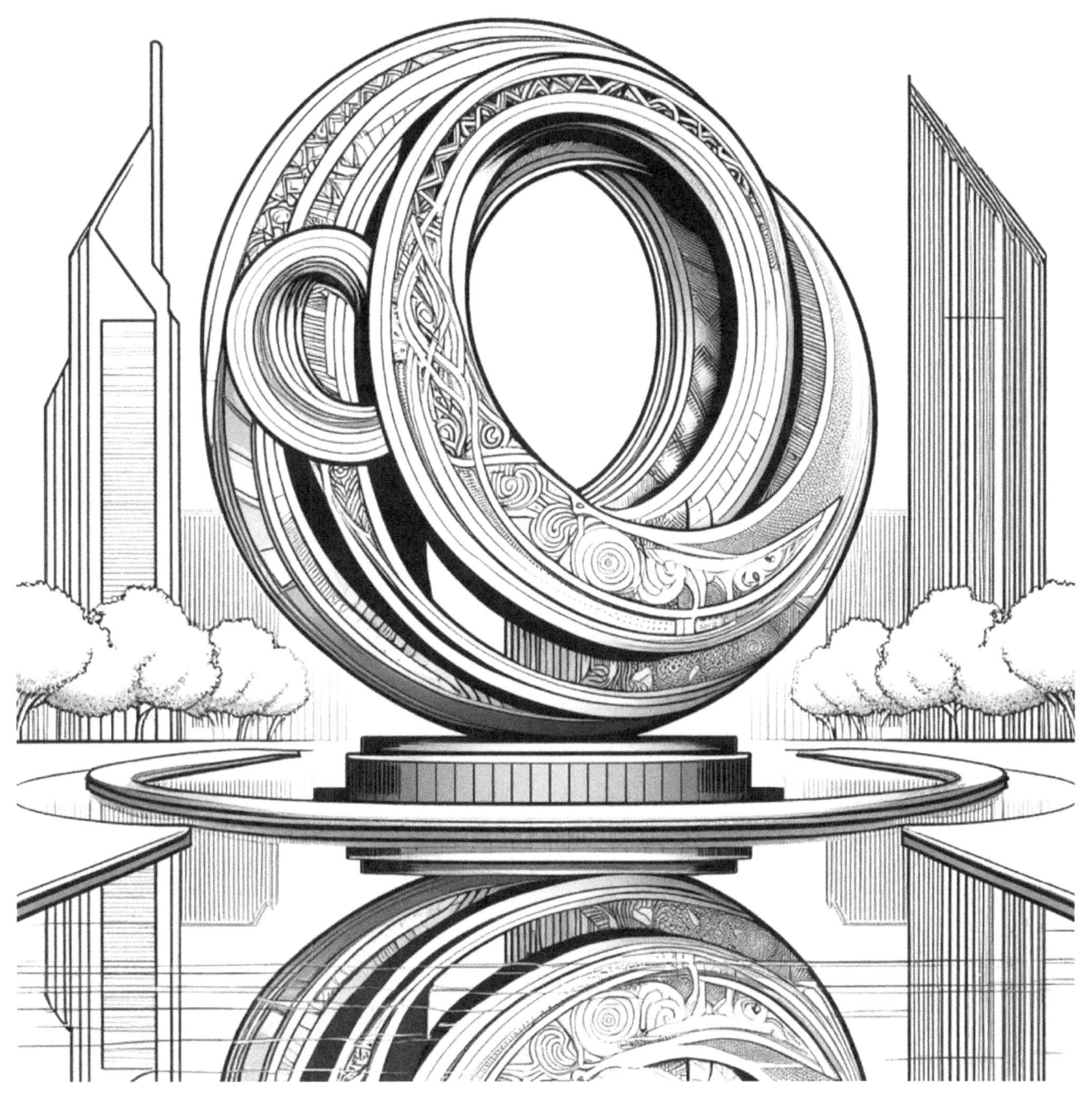

MUSEUM OF THE FUTURE.DUBAI

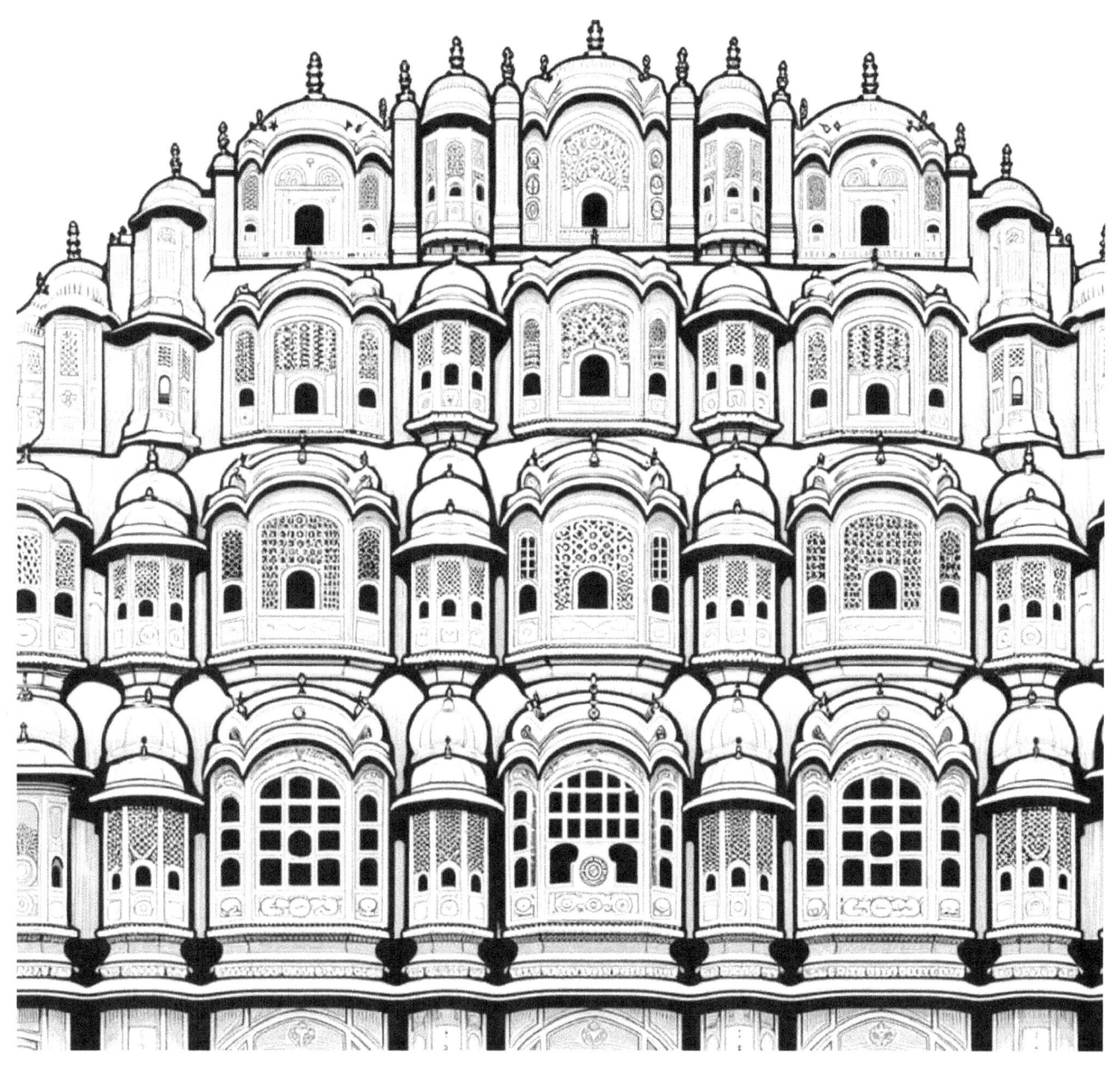

HAWA MAHAL.INDIA

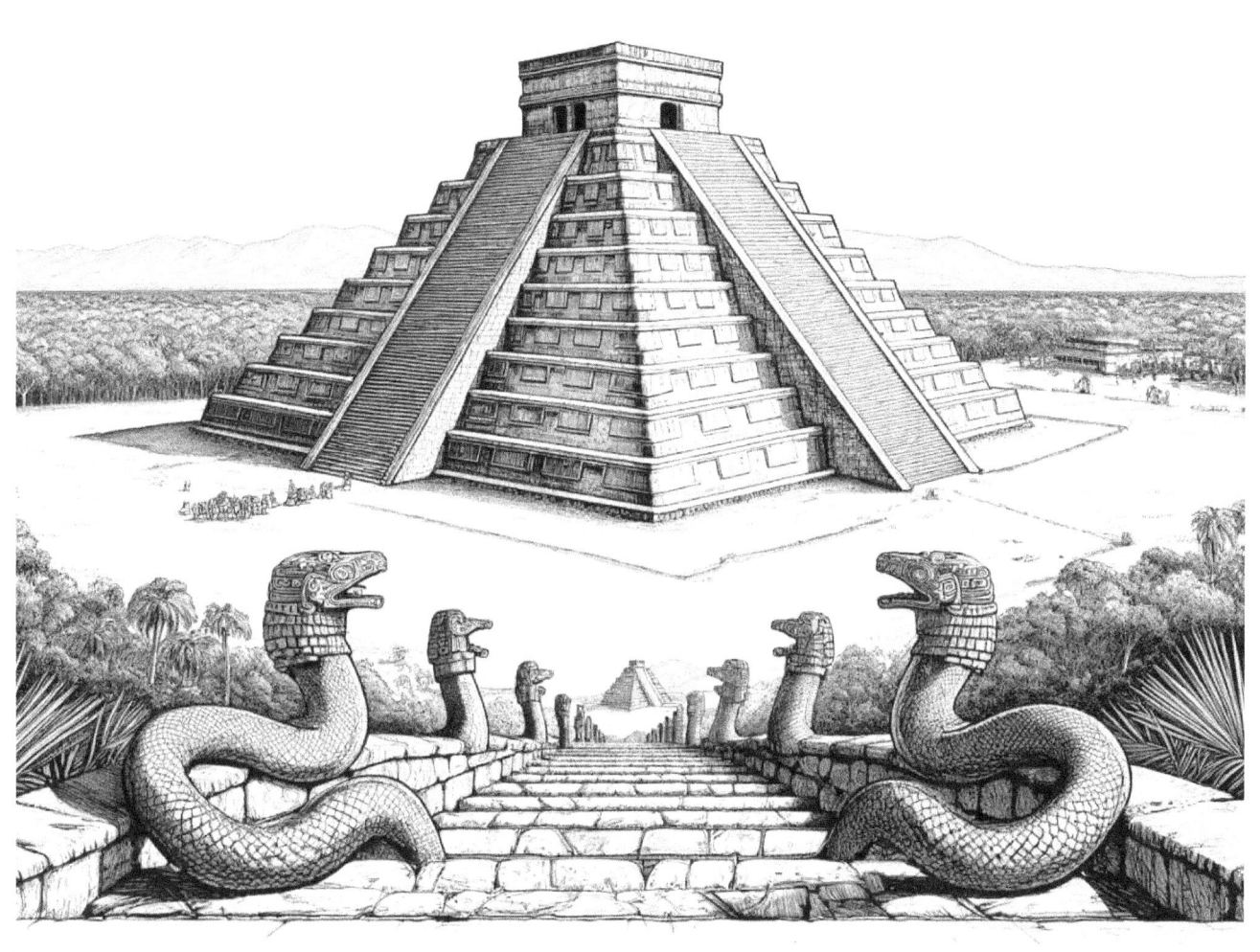

MAYA TEMPLE.MEXICO

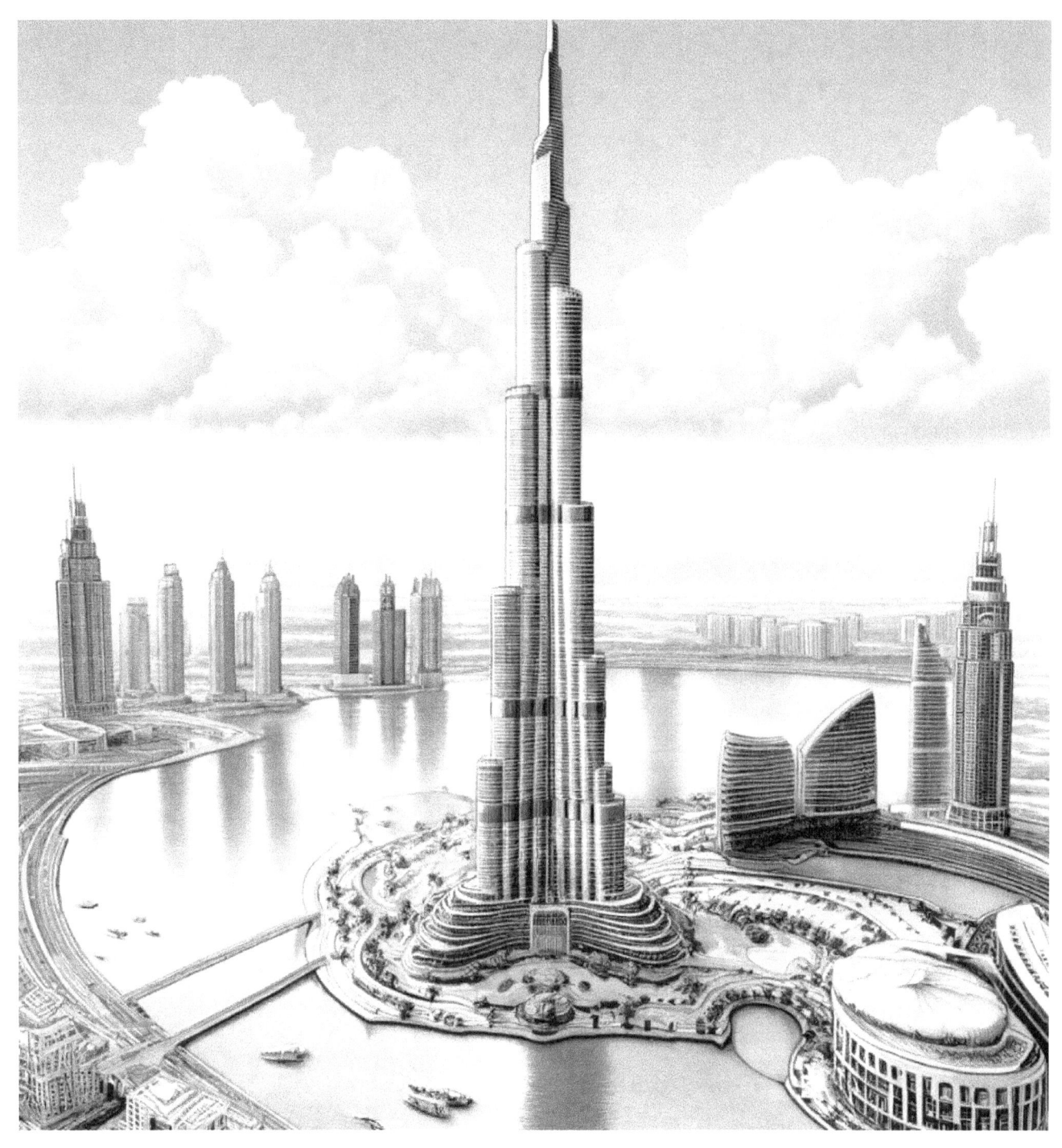

BURJ KHALIFA.DUBAI

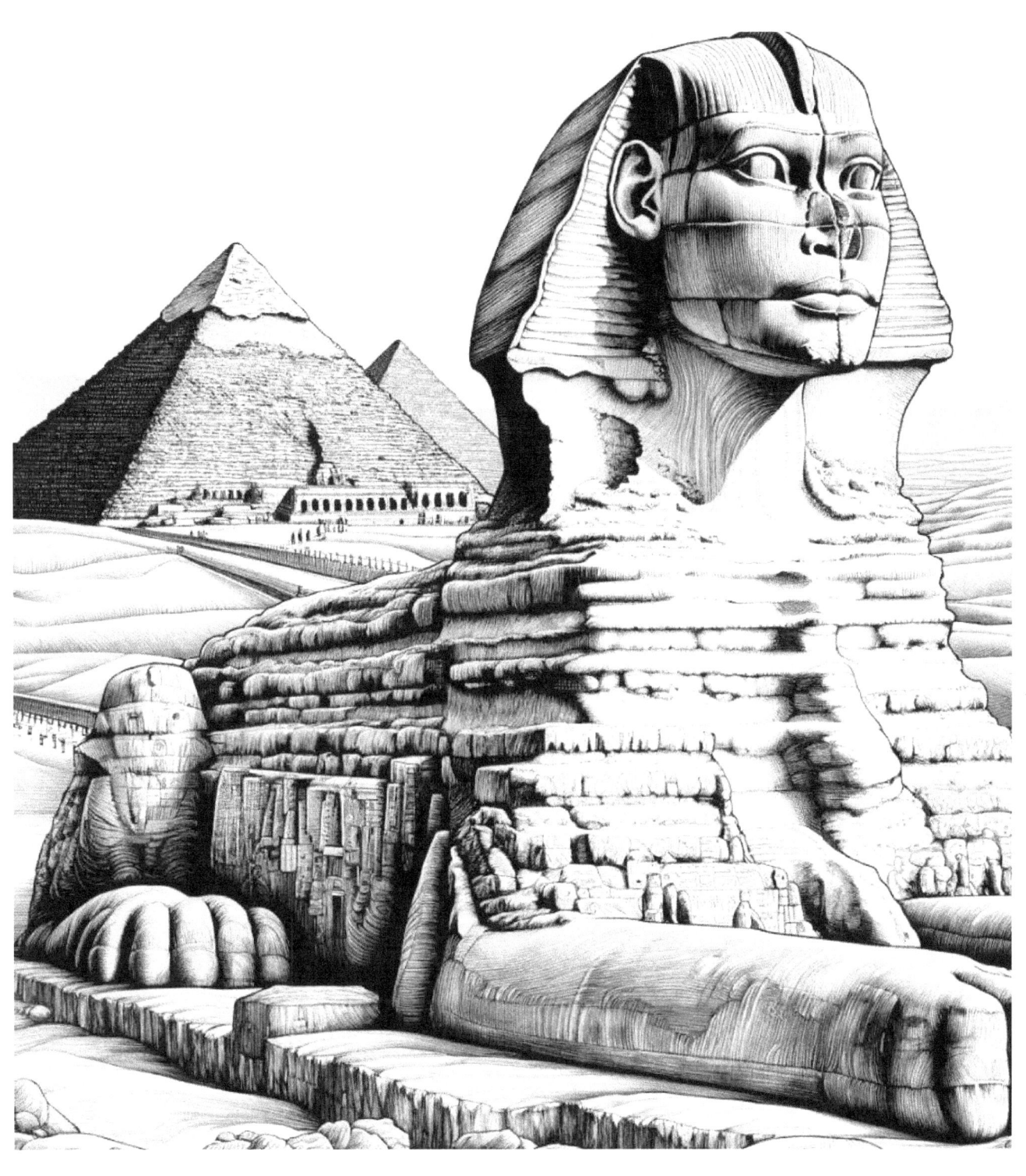

SPHINX.EGYPT

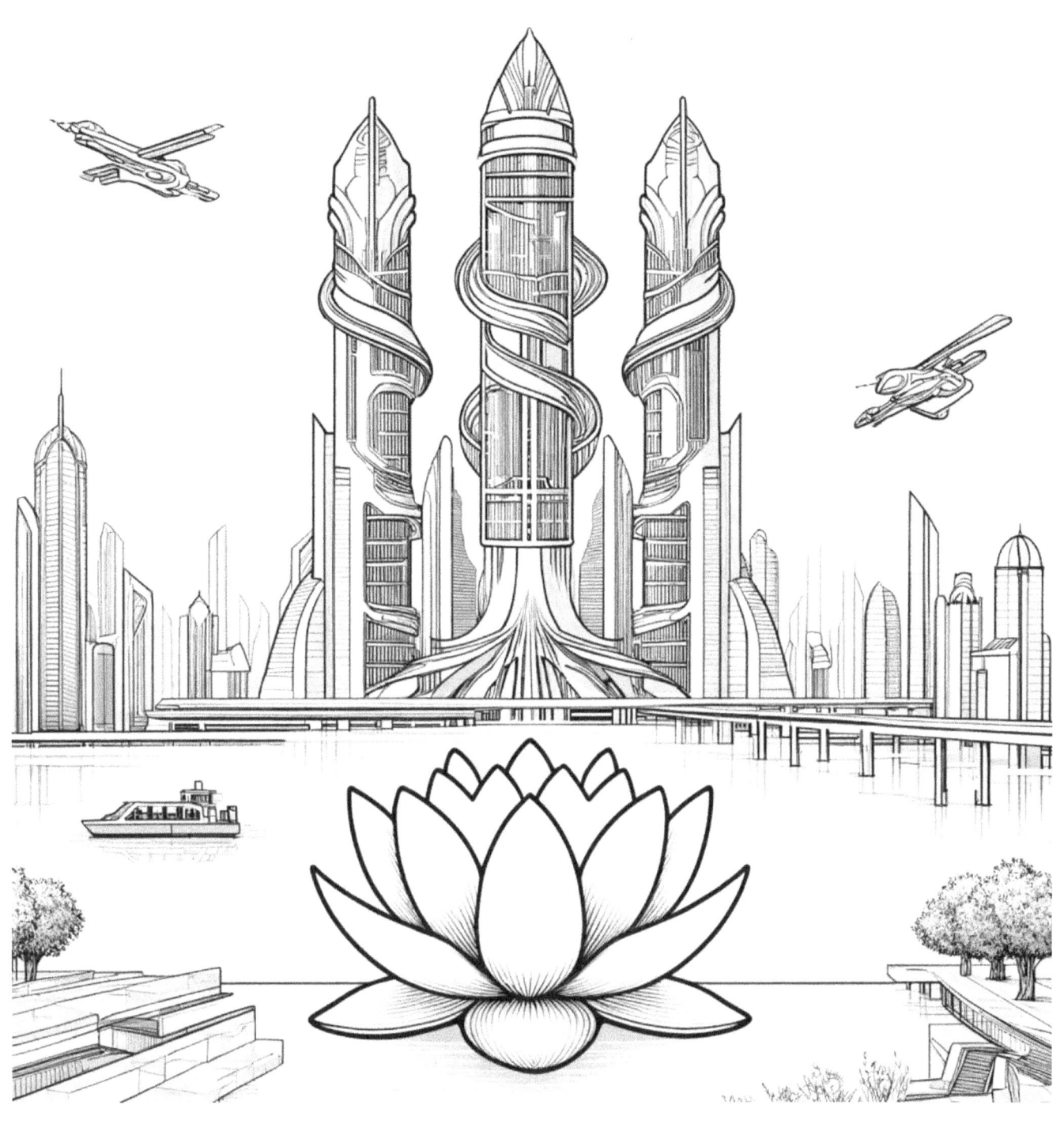

MARINA.SINGAPORE

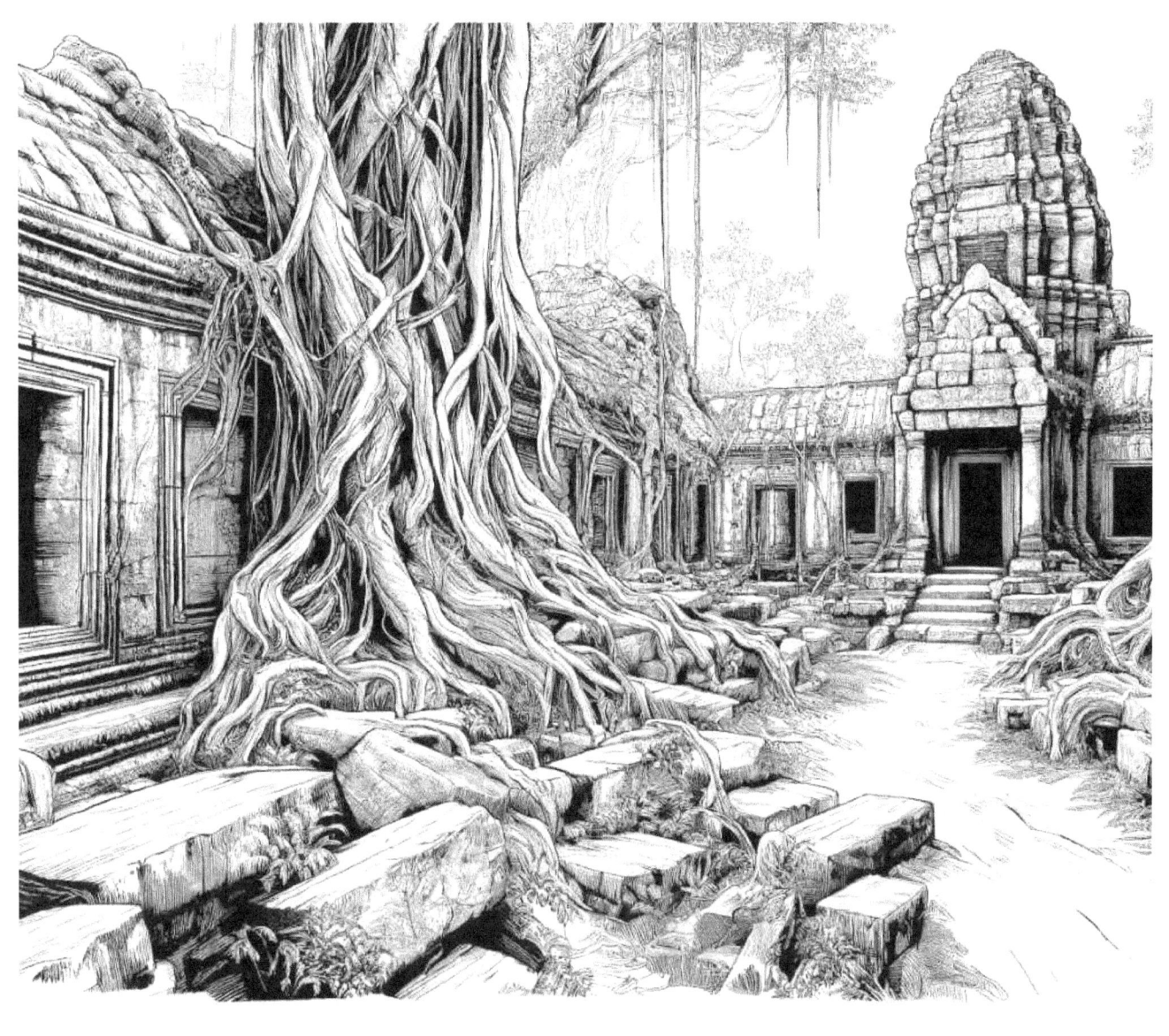

ANGKOR VAT.COMBODIA

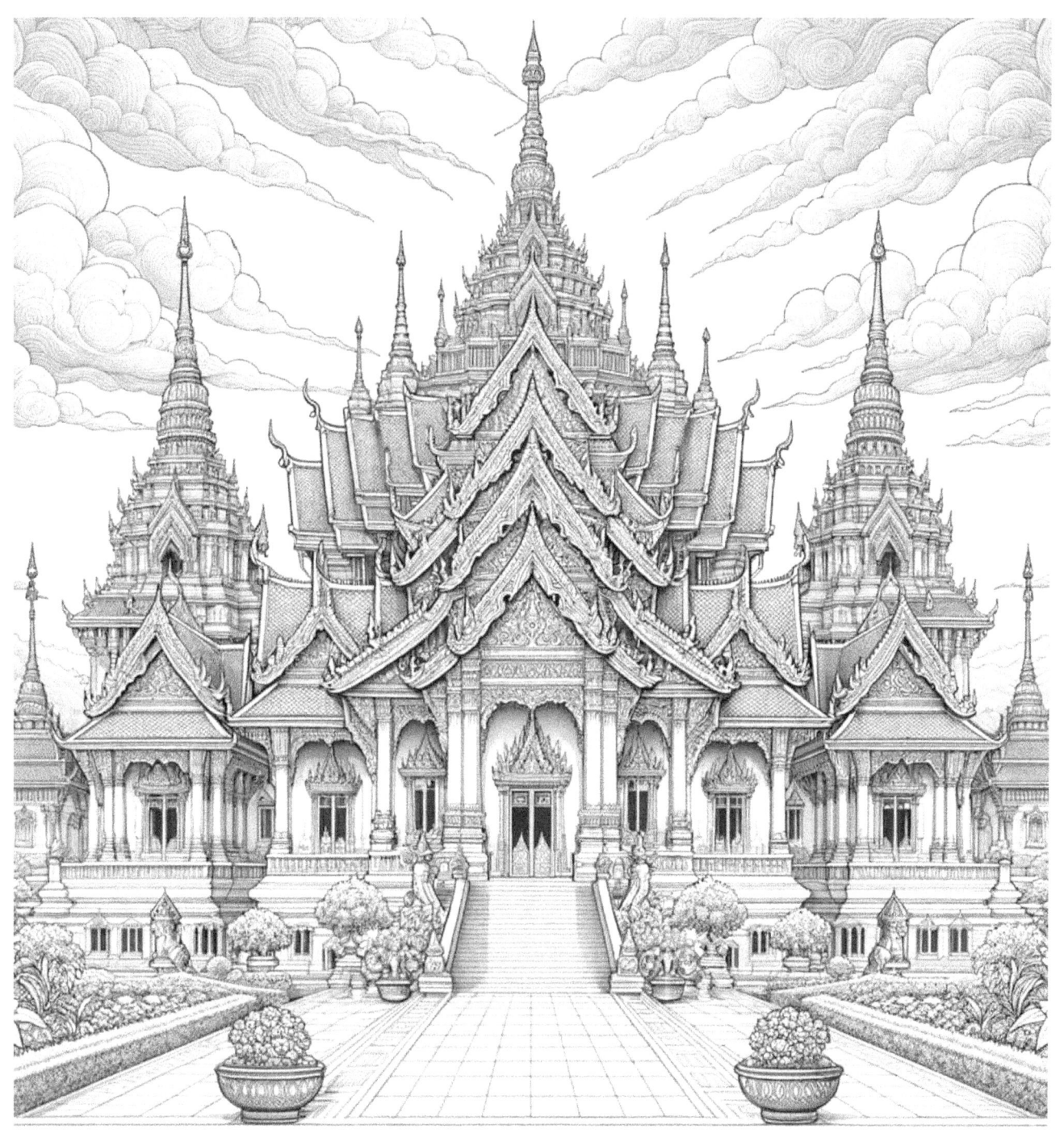

MAJESTIC TEMPLE.LAOS

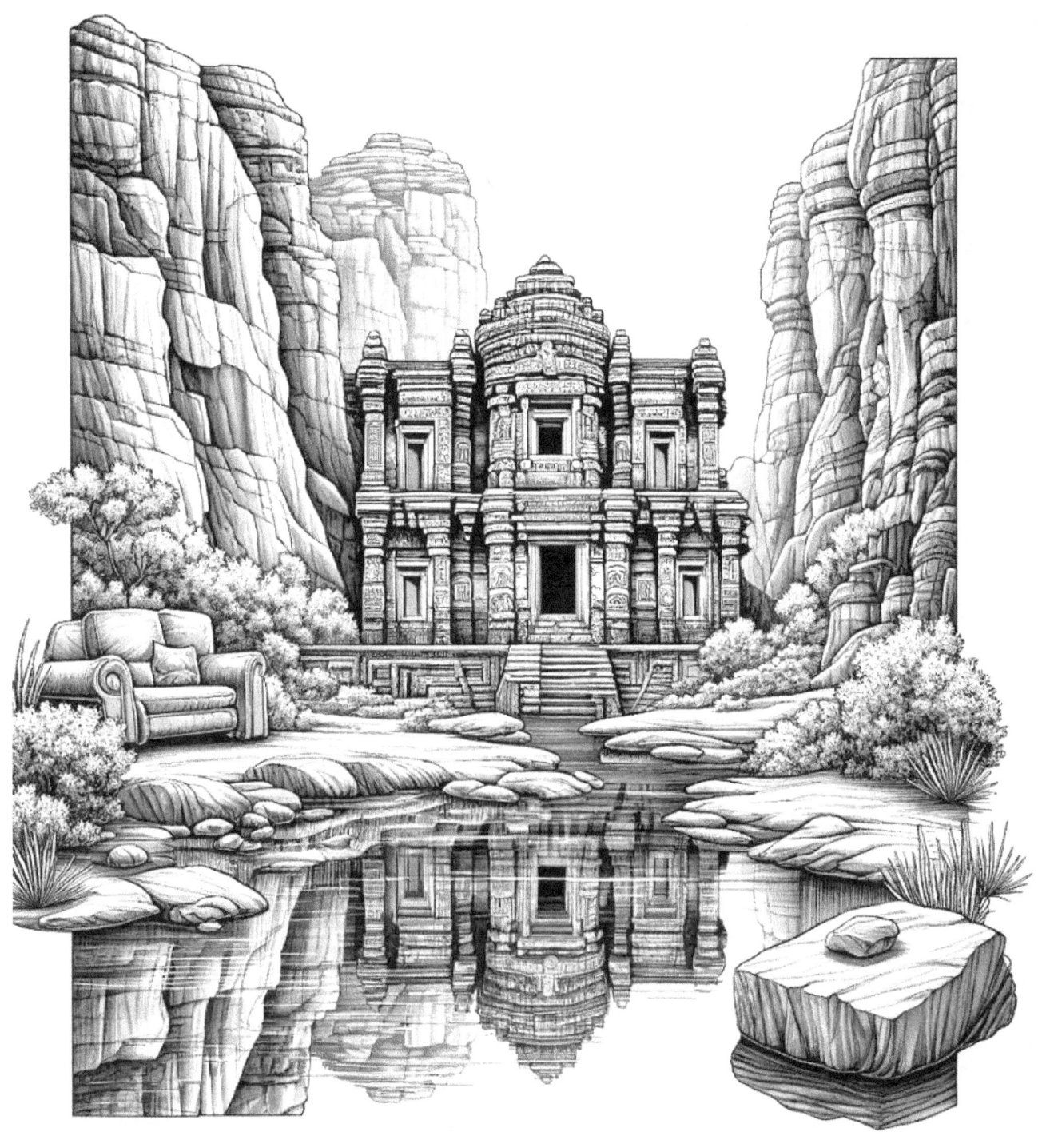

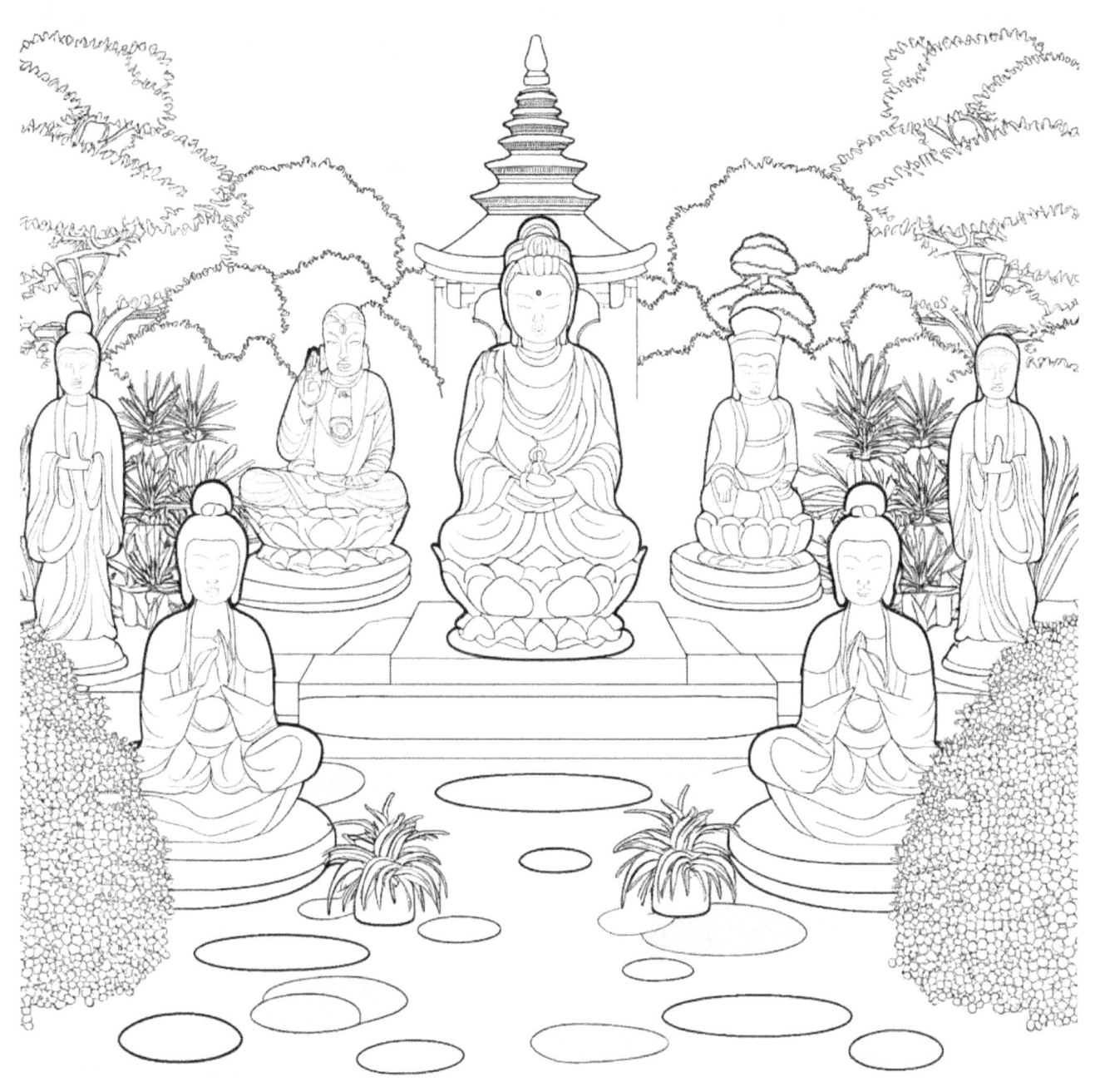

BUDDHA PARK.LAOS

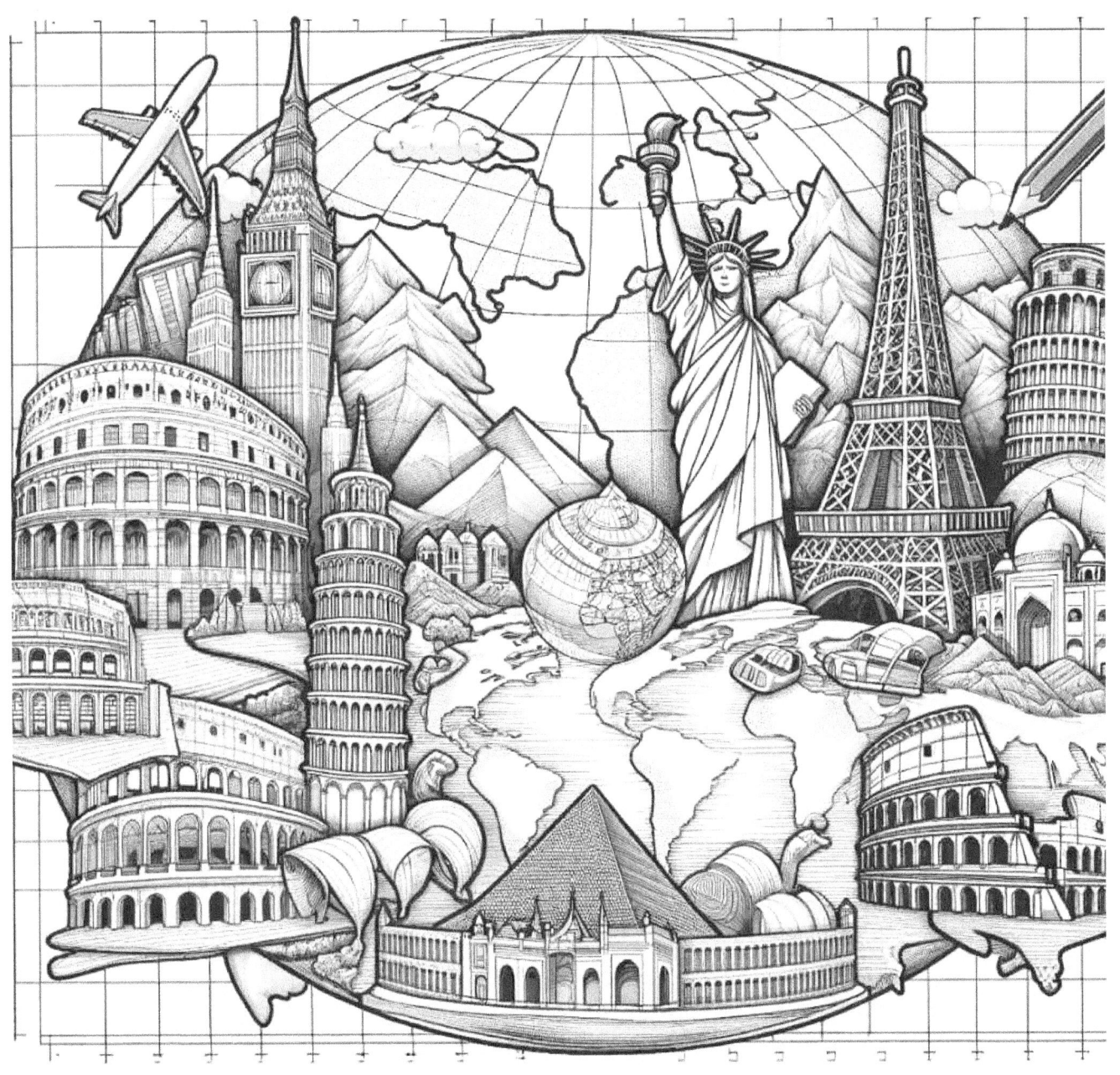

GLOBAL LANDMARKS

www.ingramcontent.com/pod-product-compliance
Lightning Source LLC
Chambersburg PA
CBHW081116240526
45470CB00020B/3116